DAIMLER AND LANCHESTER

AN ILLUSTRATED HISTORY

TONY FREEMAN

ACADEMY BOOKS

DAIMLER AND LANCHESTER

An Illustrated History

First published in Great Britain in 1990 by Academy Books
Copyright A C L Freeman
ISBN 1.873361.01.7

Printed by:
Hillman Printers (Frome) Ltd
Frome
Somerset
Tel: 0373 73526

Published by:
Academy Books
35 Pretoria Avenue
London E17 7DR

Direct sales enquiries to:
Tel: 081 521 7647
Fax: 081 503 6655

Acknowledgements

I have had much help in preparing this book from a variety of sources. Advice and assistance has come from Daimler & Lanchester Owners Club in particular, and thanks are due to David & Marie Adcock for the loan of research material, John Ridley for the loan of certain archive material, Tony Bagley, George Stapley, Keith Lanchester, Adrian Hanwell, Gresham Busby, John Pochin, Simon Pickford, Brian Long, Alex Stewart, Glenn Westwood, Brian Smith, Matthew Waterhouse, Ralph Cartwright, Chris Clarke, Mr. V. Boyd-Carpenter for their advice and assistance particularly in checking numerous details and answering many questions. The photographic department at both Jaguar in Coventry and their U S subsidiary, Jaguar Inc., are thanked, particularly Roger Clinkscales of Jaguar Cars Ltd. Karen Miller, the associate editor of Jaguar Journal. Thanks also to Les Hughes and John Bull in Australia and Gordon Sommerville in New Zealand. Thanks must go to the late Andrew Whyte, who used to write long and very detailed letters to me picking up all the errors, typographical and otherwise in *The Driving Member* shortly after I was press-ganged into editing it. Thanks are also due to Wolfgang Ansorge and Sandy Marcus for their valuable advice on the ins and outs of the publishing world. There are many other individuals too numerous to mention who have one way and another given me help, but I cannot leave out Chris Hood, who designed the book and had the unenviable task of typesetting my prose!

Tony Freeman

CONTENTS

FOREWORD

by Bill Hayden, Chairman, Jaguar Cars Limited

In **Daimler and Lanchester - an illustrated history** the author has traced the origins of both marques and chronicled their development over a period of nearly 100 years. There is a large cast of characters, as well as vehicles of all types which make this a fascinating story.

Daimler is the only British marque to have been in continuous production since the beginning of the 1890s. Lanchester ceased production in 1956 but enjoyed the distinction of being Britain's first petrol-driven four-wheeled motor car in 1895. Both Daimler and Lanchester were pioneering motor manufacturers who maintained a tradition of outstanding technical innovation and workmanship from the early beginnings in the 1890s to amalgamation in 1931.

This tradition continues through to the 1990s with the current production Daimlers, which are still regarded as amongst the world's finest luxury saloons. I am very pleased to commend this book to all those interested in the early days of the British motor industry, as well as all Daimler and Lanchester enthusiasts.

William Hayden C.B.E
Chairman and Chief Executive Jaguar Cars Limited

Introduction

The first Daimler company, Daimler Motoren Gesellschaft, was formed in Germany exactly 100 years ago by Gottlieb Daimler. Its objects were to exploit the patents filed by Daimler in Germany and, in some form, Daimler of Germany has enjoyed almost 100 years of uninterrupted trade and remains a strong independent concern which manufactures, amongst others, the Mercedes-Benz range of motor cars.

A chance meeting between Daimler and Frederick Simms at the Bremen exhibition in 1890 was the beginning of a friendship which resulted in Simms becoming a director of the German company for a short period, until 1892. Carrying out experiments on Daimler's designs, Simms realised that they had a wider application than he had first thought, and by 1893, had sufficient confidence in Daimler's patents to form an English company, The Daimler Motor Syndicate Limited. It is ironic that Simms had sufficient regard for his German colleague to name his own company after him, otherwise this book may be about the Simms company rather than the Daimler.

In contrast to the German company the English Daimler company has gone through many reincarnations and has been sold and reconstructed several times. On several occasions the Daimler marque's continued existence has been questioned, most recently following the takeover by Jaguar in 1960, the re-organisation under British Leyland in the 1970s and following the take-over of the recently privatised Jaguar by Ford in 1989.

Despite its German origins, the Daimler car is uniquely British. It was the mainstay of the Royal Mews for many years and Daimler Limousines still feature heavily in Civic fleets and the Carriage and Funeral Trades. There is something oddly eccentric about a people who can draw distinctions in social status from a mere badge, but it still happens. How many British company car parks still have spaces for the directors' Jaguars and the Chairman's Daimler? The very existence of the marque over the last 30 years has depended on this quirk, which is some indication of the goodwill attached to the name.

Lanchester, by contrast, is a name which features less and less in the collective vocabulary. Its founder, Frederick Lanchester was the designer of the first British car, which was derived entirely from first principles, and owes little, if anything, to the ideas of Lanchester's contempories in Europe and the United States. The last Lanchester was built in 1956, but the company still lingers on as a dormant, whose only outward manifestation is a small brass plate in the reception at Jaguar's Browns Lane Plant in Coventry. Whether the name will ever be revived is a question of increasing uncertainty. A marketing exercise was carried out in the early 1980s, but the public memory had faded and associations with Lancaster bombers and Burt Lancaster has made the relaunch of the marque a difficult proposition.

Yet Lanchesters were favoured amongst Royalty and Nobility in the first half of this century. George V, in particular was sufficiently taken by the marque to insist that some of the Limousines supplied to him by the Daimler Company in the 1930s be "badge-engineered" and produced as Lanchesters. More generally, Frederick Lanchester is credited with the development of many of the engineering principles which still form the basis of even the most modern cars, but nearly 45 years after his death very few outside engineering and enthusiast circles are familiar with his name.

Most of the vehicles produced by the companies have long since been scrapped, but a number of fine examples still exist, both in museums and in the hands of the membership of the Daimler & Lanchester Owners Club. Both Daimler and Lanchester were marques of high quality. Their place in the market has long since been taken by the likes of Mercedes, BMW and Jaguar.

In this book, I shall attempt to trace the origins of the companies, their development and to deal with the reasons for the demise of the Lanchester marque.

Tony Freeman
November 1990

Gottlieb Daimler.

1. GOTTLIEB DAIMLER

"No industry can have had a less encouraging or more inauspicious beginning than the motor industry of the world."

St John C Nixon
The Invention of the Automobile
1934

Mechanised road locomotion was attained as early as 1769 by Nicholas Cugnot, a Frenchman, who built a steam wagon for hauling gun carriages. In 1801, Richard Trevethick, a cornishman, constructed a full size steam road vehicle which was destroyed by fire on its first run. Undeterred, he built a second in 1803 with an enclosed coach capable of carrying four persons. This, too, had a brief life. Others, inspired by Trevethick's limited success, produced promising designs and experiments in the succeeding years and Walter Hancock even managed to introduce a passenger service in the London area. Between 1820 and 1840 these and similar vehicles performed slightly better than horse-drawn carriages and became sufficiently viable to attract the attention of other, more vested interests.

Turnpike Trusts, administered by the landed gentry, who through these trusts controlled the highways, increased toll charges to penal levels, forcing most steam coach operators out of business. At the same time, the gradual evolution of a railway system, pioneered by George Stephenson with his Stockton and Darlington Railway, soon put cheap travel within reach of the middle and working classes. As a result of this the railway network grew and the steam carriages were forgotten.

By the mid-1860s, the Railway Companies had themselves become a powerful group and were quick to act when interest in steam road vehicles was revived and experimental carriages appeared. The powerful interests threatened by these vehicles brought pressure to bear on Parliament, where three crippling acts were passed, the *Locomotive Act* of 1861, the *Locomotive Act* of 1865 and *The Highways and Locomotives (Amendments) Act* of 1878. Though the threat was more imagined than real, this notorious legislation which was to become known as the "Red Flag Acts" and restricted self-propelled "Road Locomotives" to speeds of 4 miles per hour in the country and 2 mph in towns. Each locomotive had to be attended by three people, one of whom had to walk sixty yards ahead with a red flag or warning lantern.

Thomas Alva Edison, the pioneer inventor, whose native United States was more tolerant of mechanised vehicles, stated the following opinion on this lamentable state of affairs:

> *"The motor car ought to have been British. You first invented it in the 1830s. You have roads only second to those in France. You have hundreds of thousands of skilled mechanics in your midst, but you have lost your trade by the same kind of stupid legislation and prejudice that have put you back in many departments in the electrical field."*

Edison was not wrong, for these three acts succeeded in closing Britain's roads to mechanical vehicles for nearly thirty years. As a result many important developments took place abroad.

In 1860, Etienne Lenior had patented a gas driven internal combustion engine. Simple and reliable, this engine was still being made in the late 1880s when Frederick Lanchester entered the gas engine business. Mineral fuel oil was also becoming available, yielding a liquid fuel, "benzine". In 1864, Siegfried Marcus had constructed a vehicle equipped with a primitive carburettor, but because of financial difficulties, it was never developed.

The American, George Bayton, exhibited a two-cycle stationery engine in 1876 and a second American, George Seldon filed a patent for the "American Automobile". In Germany, Nicholaus Otto developed the four-stroke engine. The induction, compression, ignition and exhaust cycle soon became the basis for "Otto's silent gas engine" refined by the firm of Otto E Langen under the supervision of its technical director, Gottlieb Daimler.

Born in Schorndorf, Wurttemburg on March 17th 1834, Gottlieb Wilhelm Daimler was the son of a baker. The elder Daimler hoped his son would become a town clerk, but the young Daimler would have none of it and as a result the boy was apprenticed to a gun maker. He was determined and ambitious and by 1857 had saved enough money to pay his way through a two year engineering course at the Polytechnic College at Stuttgart. He drifted from job to job and finally settled in a post at the Karlruhe Maschinenbaugesellschaft where he

Daimler's first car of 1886. Gottlieb Daimler is seated in the rear and his son Paul Daimler is driving. Paul Daimler was to play a significant role in the development of the Austro-Daimler company on the Continent.

remained for five years.

In 1872, looking for advancement, he accepted the position of Technical Director at Otto E Langen's engine factory. He remained there for ten years, when many improvements were introduced and the factory became the centre of interest in engineering circles in France, Belgium, England and the United States.

Amongst the many staff Daimler recruited from rival engineering firms was Wilhelm Maybach, who became Chief Designer. Together Daimler and Maybach began to address the issues involved in the eventual production of their first automobile.

By 1881, the development of gas engines was sufficiently advanced for them to be considered by Daimler as a means of providing locomotion. The original Lenior gas engines had been laughably inefficient. The gas/air mixture was not compressed before firing and fuel consumption per horsepower was lamentable. "Otto's Silent Gas Engine" was an improvement on Lenior's design, but was incapable of being run at high speed. The problem was with the ignition which consisted of a flame outside the cylinder. When the firing point was reached, a slot was opened to an outside flame which ignited the mixture inside the cylinder.

The answer to the problem lay in hot tube ignition, which had been devised as early as 1808 by Sir George Cayley and later developed in England by Watson in 1881. Using a similar system, Daimler and Maybech were able to increase the revolutions per minute of stationary gas engines. Unfortunately, the system was incapable of sustaining the high revolutions which would be required to propel road vehicles.

The solution to the problem of producing high revolutions per minute was electric ignition, first used by Lenior in 1860, and later developed by Karl Benz during 1883 and used on the first Benz internal combustion engine of 1884. Although Benz is widely credited with producing the first workable automobile in 1885, many of the features of his vehicle remained unchanged until the late 1890s, whereas Daimler and Maybach were to institute a programme of continuing development with their designs.

This began in 1882 when after visiting Russia to study the oil industry, Daimler returned to Germany and purchased a house at No. 13 Tanbeheunstrasse, Cannstatt. In the garden was a summer house and an adjoining shed. These were to serve as a workshop and a drawing office. After persuading Maybach to resign from Langen's, work began in earnest on the development of a new engine.

1891 Daimler Motor Launch with Canstatt-built Daimler engine.

Gas was supplied and Daimler and Maybach set to work, often labouring until the early hours of the morning. All this was done in secrecy and gossip began to circulate about the forging of currency. The residents of Cannstatt prevailed upon the police to apprehend the miscreants. Arming several constables the Commissioner of Police did so in the dead of night roaring with laughter when he discovered what Daimler and Maybach had really been up to.

Throughout 1883 a horizontal air-cooled engine of approximately $1/2$ HP was developed. Later, a second engine was built into their first motor cycle. This incorporated Maybach's hot tube ignition, which worked independently of the rest of the engine allowing it to attain high running speed of up to 900 rpm. A trial of a motorcycle took place on November 10, 1885, and the engine was later fitted into a small boat.

It is interesting to note that the public still regarded the internal combustion engine with an almost superstitious dread. Being powered by a highly combustious fuel, such engines were seen as a hazardous menace, in constant danger of exploding. Carrying out tests in his motor boat, Daimler found that no one would go in it as a passenger, fearing explosions. He therefore attached porcelain knobs

and insulating wire to the boat so that people would think it was driven by an electric motor!

Towards the end of 1886 a horseless carriage, powered by a single-cylinder $1^{1}/_{2}$ HP air-cooled engine with hot tube ignition was built. Later a water-cooled engine replaced this and the carriage is said to have attained the heady speed of 18 kilometers per hour on a test run from Cannstatt to Esslingen in 1887.

The vehicle was little more than a horse-drawn carriage with the shafts removed. Early on, it had been Daimler's intention to convert carriages once the new engines were accepted by the public. However, he soon realised that this was nothing but a stop-gap and in 1889 designed a vehicle from first principles, a light four-wheeled carriage with a tubular frame and a single-cylinder water-cooled engine to the rear. A third vehicle followed in 1890, but with funds running low, a company was formed to develop Daimler's patents in Germany.

The Daimler Motoren Gesellschaft was founded on 28th November 1890 with a share capital of 600,000 marks. This company was later to be the forerunner of the modern German Daimler-Benz company.

Daimler spent much of his time on the construction of motor boats and later constructed a

This is a unique photograph. On the left is the second Daimler of 1889. On the right is the Daimler motor cycle of 1884 made by Daimler and Maybach and to its left, marked "I" the first Daimler engine. In the middle is the 1000th Daimler engine and to its right the second Daimler engine. The inscription (in German) on the show stand is as follows:

"Fill the glasses to the brim,
Let us pay due homage to Labour
May the firm of Daimler have long life
Only unity leads to accomplishment."

The picture underneath the stand shows the small workshop in Stuttgart where Daimler and Maybach carried out their early research work and experiments.

small engine to power an airship. Count Zeppelin, a regular visitor to Cannstatt, constantly pressed Daimler to begin manufacturing airships. Daimler's reply to this suggestion was:

> *"People already take me for a blithering idiot because I am making horseless carriages to travel along the roads. If I tell them that I am going to fly in the air, they would consider me an uncertified lunatic!"*

An indefatigable worker, Daimler died of heart trouble on March 6th 1900, aged 66. His funeral took place on March 8th, at Uff Cemetery, Cannstatt. A small memorial was unveiled in front of the house at Cannstatt on June 1st 1902:

GOTTLIEB DAIMLER 1834-1900

"To the inventor of the Daimler engine, who in November 1885, drove his first automobile in this garden"

Daimler's contribution to automobile design in these pioneering years cannot be underestimated. Daimler designs were widely copied in Europe and the exploitation of the Daimler patents was to lead to the introduction of the Daimler car in Britain. Gottlieb Daimler is widely credited as being the inventor of the automobile (along with Karl Benz) and his influence and reputation resulted in Britain's longest surviving marque being named after him.

2. THE DAIMLER MOTOR CARRIAGE

"My Daimler Motor Carriage will stand in the window and I will create such a sensation as has never been created in London before"

H J Lawson, 1896

Frederick R Simms was born in Hamburg on August 12th, 1863. He studied patent law, became a skilled draughtsman, and was an accomplished engineer in his own right. By the age of twenty-eight, he had built a special system of aerial cableway for passenger transport. This was exhibited at Bremen in 1890. Another exhibit was a passenger trolley car which had run on narrow gauge lines from Unterbollinger and Kircheim during 1887, which was shown by a Herr Daimler and Herr Maybach.

What intrigued Simms was its means of propulsion, a small internal combustion engine capable of running at 800 rpm. Accordingly, he contacted the two exhibitors, Messrs Daimler and Maybach. He became a frequent visitor to Daimler's house at Cannstatt, and learned that the engine had been successfully tested in a motor boat and in a horseless carriage. A friendship developed with the result that Simms and Daimler were, for a time, closely associated in the management of the Daimler Motoren Geschellschaft, Simms being a director of the German firm until 1892. Eventually, an agreement was drawn up and Simms gained control of all the patent rights of the Daimler engine for the United Kingdom and the Colonies (excluding Canada).

At first, Simms concentrated on motor boats, but from 1891 to 1893 he carried out experimental work on other applications for the Daimler engine, particularly in motor vehicles. Simms had some difficulty in even exhibiting the Canstatt-built Daimler cars. In 1893, he made arrangements to show a Daimler car and a Daimler motor to run a cocoa making machine, at the German Exhibition at Earl's Court in London. The Exhibition authorities refused to allow the cocoa machine to be exhibited and claimed the law prevented the showing of the car. A proposal to run a Daimler-engined motor boat on the Serpentine was also turned down because of the fuel, benzine, which was extremely volatile.

To overcome the problems with benzine, he engaged the services of the firm of Carless, Capel and Leonard, who supplied Simms with a deodourised spirit to a specific gravity of 0.70, now popularly known as petrol.

By May 1893, he was confident that a small private company could be formed to exploit the Daimler engine and, in May 1893, *The Daimler Motor Syndicate* was formed with a capital of £6,000. At first the business went smoothly, fitting Daimler engines to launches and marketing a ticket delivery machine invented by Simms. He took a short break from managing the Company from December 1894 to April 1895, when the capital of the Company was increased to £8,000.

At this time a small but growing band of motoring enthusiasts was forming and one or two had even begun to import motor vehicles into Britain. Henry Hewetson is said to have imported a car in Autumn 1894 - a belt-driven Benz costing 1,642 marks, delivered to him in Catford. Frederick Bremer, Director of the Bremer Engineering Company of Walthamstow, London, is said to have driven a car on the roads in December 1894.

By contrast, on the continent the French, for example, encouraged and were seen to be encouraging the presence of motor vehicles on the road, the first Paris-Rouen Trial being held in 1894.

A talented public relations man, Simms was instrumental in forming the first British Motor Car Club. He is said to have invented the terms "motor car" and "petrol", and was a founder member of the Automobile Club in 1897.

Meanwhile, a Panhard and Levassor car with a Canstatt-designed Daimler engine had been imported into Britain by the Honourable Evelyn Ellis and the first motor journey over a long distance in Britain was made in defiance of the Red Flag Acts a year before their repeal. Starting from Micheldever in Hampshire and travelling from there to Datchet near Windsor, an average speed of 9.84 miles per hour was achieved over the 56 mile route and the journey completed in 5 hours and 32 minutes, excluding stops. This remarkable journey was almost certainly completed with the connivance of the individual police constables on the route. The trip attracted considerable attention, though not of the type focused on another pioneer, J H Knight, who was prosecuted for driving a motor vehicle without a traction-engine licence and for not having a man twenty yards ahead of the vehicle. This followed a short journey through Farnham, Surrey at a speed

"HORSELESS CARRIAGE" MOTORS!

"**THE ENGINEER**" says: (in Paris) "It seems that a great sale is found for the Vehicles to Country Doctors, who are able to do from forty to fifty miles a day, and in some cases the Motor has taken the place of four horses, which had to be kept previously, in order to obtain a satisfactory service."

THE DAIMLER MOTOR

COMPANY, LIMITED.

Incorporated under the Companies' Acts, 1862-1890.

CAPITAL £100,000 divided into 10,000 Shares of £10 each, *£60,000 of which is available for subscription for working Capital.* Payable 30/- on Application, £3 10/- on Allotment, and the balance in two equal monthly instalments.

Care will be taken to ensure a perfectly fair Allotment, and that no preference will be given.

"**THE DAILY TELEGRAPH**" says: "We are now on the eve apparently of a great engineering departure similar to that which produced the vast cycle industry thirty years ago—only here the possibilities are far greater. The Parisian makers are full of orders. The thing is becoming almost a craze."

Directors.

GOTTLIEB DAIMLER, Inventor of the Daimler Motor, Cannstatt, Wurtemberg.
WILLIAM WRIGHT. J.P., Moor & Robinson's Nottinghamshire Banking Co., Ltd. (Chairman of).
J. H. MACE, London Road Car Company, Ltd. (Director of).
J. J. HENRY STURMEY, Iliffe & Sturmey, Coventry.
H. E. SHERWIN HOLT, M.A., M.I.E.E., Swinburne & Company, Ltd., Electrical Engineers (Chairman of).

Bankers.

LONDON & WESTMINSTER BANK, Lothbury, E.C.

Solicitors.

J. B. PURCHASE, 11, Queen Victoria Street, E.C.
ARTHUR T. ASHWELL, Nottingham.

Consulting Engineer.

FREDERICK R. SIMMS, Billiter Buildings, 49, Leadenhall Street, E.C.

Auditors.

MONKHOUSE, GODDARD, STONEHAM & Co., 28 and 29, St. Swithin's Lane, E.C.

Secretary & Offices (pro tem.).

CHAS. OSBORN, Billiter Buildings, 49, Leadenhall Street, E.C.

The public prospectus issued for the flotation of the Daimler Motor Company in February 1896.

Prospectus for the Daimler Motor Company.

of 8 miles per hour.

Because of the constraints placed on road locomotion by the Red Flag Acts, the Daimler Motor Syndicate was compelled to road-test vehicles abroad, where the authorities were more accommodating, but Simms and his Board were confident that the British authorities could be prevailed upon to eventually repeal the 1865 and 1878 Acts.

This confidence was reflected at the Board meetings on June 7th 1895, and on July 19th 1895. At the June meeting, Simms reported that steps were to be taken to form The Daimler Motor Company for the purpose of manufacturing motor vehicles in Britain. At the July meeting, he reported that "over eighty enquiries had been received as well as many orders for carriages and offers to make the motor".

The formation of the new company commenced and arrangements were made to appoint the Hon. Evelyn Ellis as a Director, as well as Gottlieb Daimler as an Honorary Director and Consulting Engineer. This powerful combination soon attracted the attention of another pioneer, Harry Lawson.

Harry John Lawson was born in Brighton on February 23rd, 1852, the son of a puritan preacher.

The young Lawson became a student at one of Stephenson's mechanical institutions, gaining a rudimentary engineering knowledge. He was a keen cyclist and, some said, a ruthless opportunist, though he is widely credited with the invention of the chain-driven safety cycle in 1874. The bicycle made his fortune, and he floated company after company in the cycle and associated industries. A showman, with a foresight unrivalled by his contemporaries, he anticipated the development of the motor industry long before any motor vehicle could be legally driven on Britain's roads. Hoping to corner the market, he bought up every hopeful-looking patent which he could lay his hands on and in 1880 himself took out a patent for the first British motor car carrying the following description:

> "Improvements in Velocipedes and the application of Motive Power thereto, such improvements being applicable to Tram cars, Traction Engines and other Road Locomotives."

The opportunity presented by the fledgling Daimler Motor Syndicate, with its already tried and tested motor carriage, was too good to miss!

Lawson arranged for a Mr Van Praagh to call on Simms and make him an offer of £25,000 for the British Daimler motor patents, £15,000 to be made available on the spot. Simms, flabbergasted, agreed to put this before his directors, who in a short time negotiated the price up to £35,000 for the whole of the assets of the Daimler Motor Syndicate Limited - £15,000 payable immediately, which would be forfeit if Lawson could not find the balance.

The deal was concluded, Lawson and his partners formed the *British Motor Syndicate Limited*, and acquired the whole of the British Daimler patents with which they could do as they liked. By this time, Lawson's plans for exploiting the patents were well in hand and he lost little time in floating a new concern, the *Daimler Motor Company Limited*.

The prospectus was issued on Monday, February 17th, 1896. Lawson was undeterred by problems such as the use of motor vehicles on the public highway being virtually illegal, the public prejudice against the internal combustion engine, and the reluctance of some financiers to invest in anything with the Lawson name attached to it.

These obstacles were compounded by the composition of the Board named in the prospectus. It consisted of the following; Gottlieb Daimler, The Hon. Evelyn Ellis, William Wright JP, J H Sturmey, J H Mace, H E Sherwin Holt MA.

Of these, Daimler was a director in name only, he did not attend Board meetings, and from the beginning never intended and did not take any part in the affairs of the Company. The Hon. Evelyn Ellis was an enthusiast, but with no engineering

The Great Horseless Carriage Company was another of Lawson's speculations designed to exploit the Daimler patents.

experience. William Wright JP was a banker, who acknowledged his complete ignorance of all things mechanical, Sturmey was a journalist and editor of *The Autocar*. Mace was a former Director of an omnibus company, and Lawson, who was later appointed Chairman, was more of an entrepreneur than engineer despite his cycling connections.

The inexperience of the directors was to some extent offset by the appointment of F R Simms as Consulting Engineer and J S Critchley as Works Manager. Critchley was probably the most important individual in the Company at the time, being a first class engineer and one of the very few genuine automobile engineers then available.

To add to these obstacles, *The Stock Exchange Gazette* of February 15th, 1896, on hearing of the proposed flotation, anticipated what, in its view, was inevitable failure;

> *"the fact that Mr H.J Lawson is the controlling spirit is a very bad omen for the Company, and augurs a speedy acquaintance with the bankruptcy court".*

However, Lawson had not made his fortune by good luck alone. He knew that such a flotation would only succeed if he captured the public's imagination. On February 5th, he had written to Simms;

> *"I notice these expensive premises on the viaduct, with a glorious front and shop window being wasted. Why not placard it from top to bottom with "Daimler Motor Co.", and have a table with a clerk in the showroom and let the issue take place here. It is just the sort of thing we do and pay a big sum for in the City. My Daimler Motor Carriage will stand in the window and I will create such a sensation as has never been created in London before. I am quite certain that it is the right thing to do, much better than climbing to a second floor in Leadenhall Street."*

When the lists closed on the day after the issue, it was found that the public had over-subscribed by £10,000. £40,000 was paid to Lawson and his two partners of the British Motor Syndicate Limited for the Daimler patents, giving a comfortable profit of £5,000 on the original deal with Simms - £60,000 was left available for working capital. The Syndicate had obtained an option on the old Coventry Cotton Mills, a 12.5 acre site on which factory buildings had already been built at a cost of £30,000.

With premises, patents and working capital, it was time to get down to the serious business of manufacturing motor cars.

Harry J Lawson in 1896

Frederick R Simms, who is credited with the establishment of the Daimler name in Britain and a key figure in the development of the motor industry.

3. THE UNHOLY TRINITY

"One name which has not been given the attention it deserves is that of Lanchester."

Anthony Bird.
Lanchester Motor Cars, 1964.

Whilst Lawson's much publicised floatation of various motoring concerns continued through the 1890s, other key developments were carried out without any publicity. However, in terms of technical innovation, the work of the Lanchester brothers in the early and mid-1890s was probably unequalled. They are widely credited with the invention of the first all-British four-wheeled petrol-driven vehicle.

Frederick William Lanchester was born on 23rd October 1868. The son of a London architect, he was looked upon as a "rather dull boy". By his own admission, he was no sportsman (sporting achievements being given more emphasis than intelligence at certain English schools at the time). His abilities quickly became apparent when he began his technical education. He was soon joined by his brothers, Frank (born 22nd July 1870), and George (born 11th December 1874).

He was awarded a scholarship to the Royal College of Science (then the Normal School of Science and School of Mines) and augmented its limited curriculum by attending night classes at the Finsbury Technical School. After working as a hack draughtsman in Birmingham, he was able to obtain an introduction to T B Barker, a manufacturer of gas engines, and was subsequently appointed Works Manager in 1884. As early as this he demonstrated an independence of character which was to dominate his work throughout his career, when, on being presented with a draft standard-form contract of employment, he boldly struck out the clauses requiring him to assign the benefits of any inventions to his employers. To his surprise and subsequent profit, this was accepted by Barker, whose firm later benefitted from the improvements that Lanchester made to his designs. Frederick Lanchester later indentured his brother George, who was to succeed him upon his resignation from Barkers in 1893.

During his time there, Frederick rented a building adjoining the workshop where he set up a small laboratory developing high-speed gas engines. By the end of 1893, he had succeeded in building a vertical single-cylinder "high-speed" engine of around 800 rpm, most gas engines then being designed for speeds of between 150 and 200 rpm. At this time he began to turn his attentions to the theories of aerial flight, but was discouraged by Dugold Clark, a colleague, who told him;

> *"If you were seriously to propose making an engine for a flying machine you would be regarded as a crazy inventor and your reputation as a sane engineer would be ruined".*

Nearly all engineers were discouraged from seriously investigating aerial flight at this time - a great pity. However, Frederick continued with the development of a small light internal combustion engine which was installed in a motor boat. George Lanchester later recalled;

> *"The hull was designed by Fred and built by the three of us in the backyard of Fred's house in St Bernards Road, Olton, and the boat was driven by a stern paddle wheel. It was this work that earned us the title of the Unholy Trinity as the work was done mainly on Sunday's when all the neighbours were going to church or coming from it".*

Frederick Lanchester pictured in 1894, aged 26. Distracted by aeronautical research, he continued with experiments with model aeroplanes throughout the 1890s. Lanchester was a prolific inventor and filed several hundred patents relating to motor vehicles, aircraft, acoustics and mechanical engineering.

The first Lanchester car as originally built in 1895.

This first boat was launched from Salter's Yard near Oxford in the autumn of 1894. By this time, Frederick's attentions were beginning to turn towards motor car design. Only in Germany or in France could any man buy a horseless carriage, where there was a regular supply of automobiles based on Gottlieb Daimler's and Karl Benz's designs. Not impressed by these vehicles, which suffered from the twin problems of noise and vibration, Lanchester, after experiencing a number of these "boneshakers", as he described them, decided to design a motor car from scratch.

All preconceived ideas having been discarded, the vehicle was based on sound engineering principles. Both engine and bodywork would be complimentary and the first experimental car contained a number of innovative design features.

The design work was carried out during 1894, and construction of the first Lanchester car began in 1895. Work progressed slowly, both because Fred was distracted by his aeronautical research, and because of his refusal to compromise and use readily available components, which he considered unsuitable.

The result was a remarkably advanced design. Some of the features of this first car are incorporated in todays modern vehicles, such as the use of live axles, mechanically-operated inlet valves, low-tension ignition and oil filtration. The engine was placed in the middle of the frame, with the single-cylinder air-cooled 5HP engine inclined 30 degrees horizontally in a forward position. Gear-changing was by pedal with the weight of the foot, and speed

was regulated by a "knee swell" an arrangement which resembled the volume control on a church organ. The carburettor, which was integral to the fuel tank, was a hand-operated cotton-wick type, variations of which were used in most Lanchester cars until 1914. The car was tested under cover of darkness sometime in February or March 1896 by Frederick and George Lanchester. It soon became clear that the car was underpowered, being only capable of 15mph on level ground, driver and passenger having to disembark to push the vehicle up even the gentlest of inclines, and the car was later converted to a twin-cylinder 8HP engine and fitted with the first Lanchester worm gear.

In its redesigned form, the car easily made journeys of 100 miles or more, averaging 12mph with a maximum speed of 18mph. This vehicle became the demonstration car with which the brothers, particularly Frank Lanchester, whose diplomatic and marketing skills were quickly developing, canvassed backers in order to commence production. Writing in 1948, George Lanchester noted that:

> "...half a century ago, we had no accumulated data on the many problems connected with road locomotion - the effect of load, road surface coupled with what was then high speed - were imperfectly understood, and in spite of careful application of scientific principles and theories, much had to be deduced from trial and error."

16

With the body removed, the engine layout in the middle of the frame is clearly seen. This is in contrast to the layout used in the majority of the early cars imported from France and Germany, which were largely based on Daimler and Benz's designs. The tiller is a Lanchester innovation since it faces forward and corrects the inherently dangerous instability of the "bath chair" type tiller used elsewhere.

The car as rebuilt, with twin-cylinder 8HP engine, Lanchester worm gear, hood and wheel steering.

Lanchester's second car, pictured shortly after construction. Frederick Lanchester is driving with brother George as passenger. The car is now preserved in the Science Museum, South Kensington, London.

Fred himself recalled:

> *"We believed in those days that the motor car would replace the horse vehicle - not the railway train - and we were thinking of speeds of about 15 mph."*

A second, higher-powered vehicle was designed, and work on this began in earnest in 1896.

A syndicate headed by the Whitfield brothers was formed to finance and develop Lanchester's patents, and a more spacious work shop was found at Ladywood Road in Birmingham. The introduction of a completely new design and production process required the recruitment and training of skilled workmen and time was spent designing and equipping a workshop which would be capable of producing the Lanchester designs.

By the time the first car was rebuilt in 1897, the Locomotives on Highways Act of 1896 had been passed, repealing the Red Flag Acts and speeds of up to 12mph were permitted. The second car (later known as the Gold Medal Phaeton), was built, though this took a long time, even by the standards of the day. Again, Lanchester returned to his first principles, even re-designing nuts and bolts, and evolving a primitive quality control system, which

allowed for the use of interchangable parts between vehicles.

The maximum speed of this second car was 30 mph, very fast by the standards of 1898. The design was advanced and the ride smooth, but Fred and George soon tired of running it round the block, constantly on the watch for policemen and set off on a non-stop run of 68 miles, averaging 26 mph. However, apart from the occasional appearance by one or the other brothers in the Magistrates Courts in Birmingham, no attempt was made to publicise the car or to raise further finance by the Lanchester syndicate.

Commenting on this in *Britain's Motor Industry* in 1950, George Lanchester recalled:

> *"Reference to the motor journals of the period reveals little, if any information about Lanchester car, and excepting an article published in an obscure little journal called Our City, published in Birmingham, and long since defunct, I cannot recall any press publicity until 1899, when the two-seat Phaeton of 1898 was entered and driven by Fred in the Richmond Show and Motor Trials, and was awarded a gold medal for its design and performance. 'The*

Gold Medal Phaeton' as it was called, is now in the safe keeping of the Science Museum, South Kensington...We never sought publicity for the good reason that we were not yet manufacturing cars for sale."

By the time a third car was being assembled in 1898, a production design had been finalised, and the decision was made to form a company and go into the business of selling these motor cars. The second car was driven to London and entered in the Automobile Club's Reliability Trial and Exhibition at Richmond in June 1899. Of only two "Special Gold Medals" awarded by the Judges, Lanchester's was for "excellence of design".

Although *The Autocar, The Auto Motor,* and the RAC's own publication gave little space to the Lanchester "Passenger Spirit Phaeton" (hardly surprising really, as *The Autocar* was then edited by Henry Sturmey - a Director of the Daimler Motor Co. Limited), a detailed report appeared in *The Times* newspaper;

"A motor carriage has recently been introduced by Mr F W Lanchester of Birmingham, which has distinct improvements over other forms of vehicle of this nature... the motor is a two-cylinder oil engine working on the Otto cycle and occupies a central position well out of sight. The most salient features of novelty occur in this motor, the principal departure from previous practice existing in the means taken to avoid vibration, one of the chief objections to ordinary motor cars driven by oil engines. The result of Mr Lanchester's invention has been to produce an exceptionally easy running carriage equal in fact to one electrically driven whilst the steering and manoeuvring qualities are quite remarkable. We are informed that the carriage made the journey to London in 6 ½ hours running time."

It is interesting to note that the time recorded is exactly the time it would have taken if the then national speed limit of 12mph had been exactly the average speed! Following the Reliability Trials, in fact, the speed at which the car completed the journey was well above that average, but Frederick Lanchester often made a well-documented practice of a stopping, prior to reaching his destination, allowing the passage of time to reduce the average speed, and thus avoid prosecution for speeding!

In the meantime, Frank Lanchester continued in his efforts to raise capital for the formation of the Company. On the 27th October 1899, the formation was announced in "The Motor Car Journal" of The Lanchester Engine Company Limited, which was finally incorporated on 13th December, 1899.

The Lanchester Gold Medal Phaeton seen here on a hill-climbing test at Deer Park, Richmond, in June 1899.

4. PROBLEMS, PROBLEMS, PROBLEMS!

"Important matters have been constantly deferred and the business of the Company has not been conducted in the efficient and energetic manner which is so indispensable for the success of any commercial enterprise."

Arthur Rawlingson.
Daimler Shareholder, 1898.

Thanks to the authorities' attitude to "road locomotion", very little in the way of automotive engineering expertise existed in Britain in 1896, least of all amongst the esteemed Directors of the Daimler Motor Company. Accordingly, they decided to visit the leading French and German concerns to see for themselves how to go about the formidable task they had set themselves. By their return, Lawson's syndicate had acquired two disused factories in Coventry which were deemed suitable for the proposed manufacture of motor carriages.

It is often thought that the Company's premises in Coventry were acquired by chance. In fact, mere luck had very little to do with it. On 20th May 1896 in *The Financial News* Lawson had informed shareholders that:

> *"We did not wish to build works because it would take too long, so we visited various works in the country which were for sale. We went to Cheltenham and Birmingham, in both of which places (sic) there were no Motor Works for sale... At last we went to Coventry, and we saw what we believed to be an almost perfect place for manufacturing these machines."*

Behind all this optimism and the rationalisations, it is more than likely that Lawson had had his doubts about the viability of this venture. There is evidence that he hedged his bets quite carefully. For example, he stressed that the Company would be based in Coventry. This was not an arbitrary choice. Coventry had been associated with the cycle boom of the 1880s and continued to be a successful and profitable centre for cycle production. As a result, there was an experienced and skilled labour force to draw upon as well as an established components industry.

This site comprised 12 acres at first, but part was soon sold to other Lawson concerns. It comprised of a number of good quality buildings and was close to both inland waterways and railway facilities. However, Coventry was not unique in this respect and it is indeed likely that other suitable premises were available. What was certain was Harry Lawson

had numerous friends and business contacts in the Coventry area, having first arrived there in the 1870s to work in the cycle industry.

Amongst these contacts was Henry Sturmey, editor of *The Cyclist* and later *The Autocar*. Sturmey's friendship with Lawson was important in that he was his chief ally through the pages of *The Autocar*, and had invested quite heavily in the initial flotation of the Company and was well placed to chair Board meetings when Lawson was otherwise engaged in negotiating other business deals. *The Autocar* effectively became the main advertising medium for the new Daimlers and provided a mouthpiece for replying to Lawson's critics.

A third element contributed to the choice of premises. There was considerable competition amongst the local banks to secure the custom of new motor manufacturing concerns. This was due to a slump in the cycle manufacturing industry which worsened towards the end of the 1890s. With no immediate outlet for funds the banks were prepared to be more accommodating to the new venture, whoever had promoted it, than would have otherwise been the case in any other city at the time.

Lawson had turned his attentions to the floating of yet another public company - the so-called *Great Horseless Carriage Company Limited*. Again, the aim was to exploit the Daimler patents, now acquiring the quite astonishing value of half-a-million pounds, to be paid to the *British Motor Syndicate Limited*, which was of course controlled by Lawson. This would, according to the prospectus, be paid for out of the proceeds of the issue of three-quarters of a million pounds worth of shares in yet another flotation!

The Press were not slow in seeing through Lawson's schemes and the *Pall Mall Gazette* published a scathing attack on the Daimler Motor Company Limited, accusing the Directors of "careering around Europe in search of motor knowledge and spending half the capital of the Company before serious work was started." It also unkindly drew attention to the falling value of Daimler shares.

Other critics chose to attack Harry Lawson on the latest of his company promotion schemes, many

A line-up of early Daimlers with many of the personalities involved in the early Daimler Company.
From left to right;
The Hon. Evelyn Ellis, a director of Daimler and importer of a Canstatt Daimler-engined Panhard & Levassor in 1895. Also in the car are J Barstow JP and Mrs Barstow of Weston-super-Mare.
In the second car is driver Charles Osbourne, Secretary of the British Motor Syndicate and at one time Harry Lawson's right-hand man. Seated next to him is Crompton, an employee.
In the third car, Charles Harrington-Moore is driving, the first Secretary of the Royal Automobile Club, J S Critchley, Daimler works manager, and F R Simms, first consulting engineer of Daimler.
The fourth car is a Benz, imported by Harry Hewetson in 1894. He can be seen in the rear seat.
The fifth car is driven by Tom Lawson, eldest son of Harry.
J H Mace, a Daimler director is in the sixth car.
In the seventh car is Harry Lawson himself, first Chairman of Daimler.

of which were said to have been designed only to exploit gullible and greedy investors. One of the sternest critics was *The Economist*:

> *"Mr Lawson is still a comparatively young man, and it is only in the past ten years, we believe, that he discovered his genius for piling nominal capitalisation out of small beginnings, and his fertility for placing shares among enterprising investors. But short as is the period of Mr Lawson's promotions, it has proved much too long for most of them. Many have long since been buried and almost forgotten, except by the surviving sufferers; others have been reconstructed over and over again, and have at last got free from the control of their author, while in some instances there have been mysterious disappearances."*

The *Autocar* magazine launched a petition to legalise the use of motor vehicles of the highway's without the obligatory pedestrian carrying a red flag and an exhibition was arranged at the Imperial Institute from May 9th to August 9th, 1896.

The exhibits were fitted with imported engines, and were listed as follows:

> *Two "neat little cars" with Benz engine, by the Arnold Motor Carriage Company, of 59 Mark Lane, London.*

> *A 4-wheeled, electrically-driven dogcart by Offord and Sons, of 92 Gloucester Road, London.*

> *A phaeton and a landau, electrically-driven, by Walter Bersey (The Universal Electric Carriage Co., of 39 Victoria St., London). Several Cars by the Daimler Motor Company Ltd., of 40 Holborn Viaduct, London, and Coventry.*

The Editor respectfully requests that all interested in the autocar movement will sign and kindly assist by obtaining signatures to the following petition, returning the same to him at earliest possible date, but not later than February 25th, addressed—"The Autocar" Office, 19, Hertford Street, Coventry.

SESSION, 1896.

TO THE HONOURABLE THE COMMONS OF THE UNITED KINGDOM OF GREAT BRITAIN AND IRELAND IN PARLIAMENT ASSEMBLED.

THE HUMBLE PETITION of the undersigned

SHEWETH as follows:

1. That great attention has lately been devoted to the improvement and development of horseless carriages for passenger and other uses, and that a considerable industry in the manufacture of such carriages has arisen in other countries, and that capital has been subscribed, and money expended, with a view to introduce and develop a like industry in this kingdom.

2. That the statutory enactments relating to highways and regulating the use of locomotives (which description has been held to include the above-mentioned carriages) upon the turnpike or other roads in this kingdom are entirely inapplicable and obstructive to the user of all such horseless carriages, and that thereby the industry of manufacturing such carriages is retarded, and further development in the scientific construction of the same is discouraged.

Your petitioners therefore humbly pray your Honourable House that such changes in the law may be effected as shall remove the above grievances.

The petition to repeal The Highways and Locomotives (Amendment) Act of 1878 sponsored by The Autocar. When the amending legislation was finally passed, The Autocar printed a commemorative issue in red.

The Emancipation Run of November 1896 was organised by Harry Lawson to commemorate the repeal of the despised Red Flag Acts. Here he is seen in Brighton (in the foreground), on Saturday November 14th, 1896.

The car in the foreground is an imported Benz car. In the rear vehicle is Gottlieb Daimler, who despite failing health travelled in a car driven by Frederick Simms.

A carriage frame for the Daimler motor chassis, by Mulliners, of Birmingham.

A vehicle with Kane-Pennington engine by the British Motor Syndicate, of Coventry.

Some authorities were becoming more optimistic about the future of the motor vehicle and the exhibition went some way towards generating the favourable publicity needed for the Company's future development. *The Financial News* of May 1896 stated that:

"It is never safe to prophecy, but it seems as if we are on the eve of the inauguration of a very great industry, which will not only be profitable in itself, but will augment the profits of innumerable other industries. That horseless carriages have passed out of

the purely experimental stage, any visitor to the Imperial Institute may see for himself."

The Prince of Wales, later King Edward VII, had been given a private demonstration on February 14th by the Hon. Evelyn Ellis, driving F R Simms' Cannstatt Daimler. It is said that the Prince, bringing his considerable influence to bear, was able to turn the tide of establishment opinion on the motor car by making it fashionable.

Within a short space of time, *The Locomotives on Highways Act, 1896* was passed, repealing the previous legislation and raising the speed limit to a, what was then, more realistic maximum of 12 mph.

The Autocar celebrated the occasion by printing its current issue using red ink!

Lawson lost no time in organising a publicity stunt, the Emancipation Run from London to Brighton, and this took place on Saturday, November 14th, 1896. Many Daimler-engined cars

23

TWO-SEATED CARRIAGE, WITH HOOD AND DETACHABLE FRONT ... £216

FOUR-SEATED PRIVATE OMNIBUS, WITH SEPARATE SEAT FOR DRIVER ... £295

were in evidence, as well as a strong contingent of British Daimler Company staff. Gottlieb Daimler himself was in attendance, despite his failing health, riding in a car driven by F R Simms.

58 entries were received for the run, which though widely reported and celebrated, proved to be somewhat deficient in other respects. St John Nixon, writing in 1961 commented as follows:

> "The "Emancipation" run of November 1986 was so extremely badly organised and conducted that no one knows what actual vehicles took part, apart from about a dozen which have been established. More than one joined the procession half way, whilst at least one electric car was taken to Brighton by train, made to look dirty and then run about Brighton as though it had come by road."

In the meantime, the Daimler Motor Company issued catalogues with imaginative drawings of what they hoped the first British Daimler cars would look like and attempted to establish production at the Coventry factory. Even though manufacturing techniques were being developed from first principles, it took some three to four months to produce a complete car.

In July 1897 Evelyn Ellis and J S Critchley took a car to Malvern Beacon, where with Ellis' daughter as passenger they reached the top of this very steep hill. 23 minutes and 2 1/2 miles took them 800 feet above sea level, a second stage took them a further mile and 640 feet up the hill. Overall the journey had a gradient of 1 in 4 1/2 to 5 3/4. More than mere showmanship, this demonstrated reliability and performance in difficult road conditions.

In the summer of 1897, Major-General Montgomery of Winchester placed the first order from a private customer for any car built in the United Kingdom. By this time, the Company was so far behind in its promised times for deliveries, that the car intended for Henry Sturmey's planned proving run from John O'Groats to Lands End was delayed and the car delivered to the Major-General, and Sturmey had to wait until October before commencing his famous run. By late summer a second car was prepared and in September 1897 it

The 1896 Daimler Company catalogue contained many imaginative drawings of what it was hoped the cars would look like. In fact the commencement of production was continually delayed, and the first cars were not delivered to customers until late 1897.

THE DAIMLER MOTOR SYNDICATE, LIMITED,

95, BILLITER BUILDINGS,
49, LEADENHALL STREET,
LONDON, E.C.

First Prize
Motor-Carriage Competition,
PARIS, 1894 AND 1895.

FOUR-SEATED OMNIBUS £270

THE DAIMLER MOTOR SYNDICATE, LIMITED,

Engineers,

95, BILLITER BUILDINGS, 49, LEADENHALL STREET,

LONDON, E.C.

Telegraphic Address—"DAIMLER LONDON."

THE DAIMLER PETROL-MOTOR CARRIAGE.

TYPES.—Carriages are made in various types and designs, a variety of which is shown in the accompanying illustrations. They are constructed to accommodate either two, four, or six persons, or more if required. A tender in the form of a small two-wheeled or other suitable vehicle may be attached.

MOTOR.—The Carriages are propelled by our Daimler Patent Oil Motor with two Cylinders. The Motor is either placed in the front or rear of the carriage, and is easily accessible from all sides. The construction of the Motor being extremely simple, enables any intelligent person, without previous technical knowledge, to soon become expert in the working of both the Motor and Carriage, as well as keeping same in proper order. The lubrication also is easily effected. The Engine does not emit any offensive smell, smoke, or heat, and can be started within two or three minutes. The great feature of the Daimler Motor, which is constructed on the same principle as any ordinary gas engine, is its safety and reliability, thus avoiding the slightest danger of explosion.

STEERING.—The Steering is effected by a lever, easily worked by the left hand, causing no fatigue even on a long run. The right hand and feet work certain other levers for putting the engine in and out of gear, varying the speed, going forward or backward, as well as actuating the brakes whenever necessary.

SPEED.—The four speeds may be varied according to circumstances, the average travelling velocity being about 8 to 12 miles in the open, and may even be increased to 15 miles per hour, and more on a clear road. The highest speed is generally employed on the level, and the lowest when mounting hills or going over bad roads, as then more power is required. The Daimler Motor-Carriage easily overcomes gradients—1 in 10, even on a long ascent—the uphill speed varying from 3 to 7 miles.

BRAKES.—Two powerful independent Brakes are provided, one being worked by a foot—the other by a hand lever; the latter only being employed on very steep hills, or where an immediate stop may become necessary

FUEL.—As fuel, rectified Petroleum (Petrol or Benzoline) of 0·680 to 0·705 specific gravity is used, having many advantages over common petroleum, and being obtainable almost anywhere. The fuel is stored in two closed metallic reservoirs, which are under no pressure, and from one of which the Motor feeds itself automatically. The vessel near the engine contains sufficient fuel for a 35 mile run, whereas the supplementary tank, generally placed in the rear of the carriage, contains enough for about 120 miles.

WATER.—The cooling water required for keeping the cylinders at the right temperature is carried in a small tank, or part of same in the hollow tubular framework of the carriage, and has to be renewed every 25 to 30 miles.

CONSUMPTION.—The consumption varies according to the horse-power of the engine, the number of passengers, as well as the condition of the roads. A two-seated carriage costs about a halfpenny per mile, and a four-seated vehicle under three farthings.

GENERAL DETAILS.—We supply our Carriages, painted and varnished, ready for use. Each carriage is carefully tested by a run of at least 60 miles previous to delivery. The upholstering is either in drap or in maroquin, as may be desired. The wheels are of well-seasoned wood with iron tyres, and specially suitable for continuous, long, and hard use. At a moderate extra charge we also supply wheels with rubber tyres, which will naturally ensure smoother travelling as well as causing less strain on the engine. The body of the carriage is mounted on superior springs, and the cushions being likewise very elastic and comfortable, the traveller can undertake long journeys without the slightest fatigue. Our Carriages are also fitted, if required, with folding hoods, or any other suitable covering; they are of superior and elegant finish, only the best materials being employed. All necessary tools are included.

TERMS.—The prices of our Carriages are net cash, ex London, one-third with order, one-third on commencement of fitting Motor, balance on delivery, or according to special arrangement.

GUARANTEE.—We guarantee our Carriages for three months after delivery in such a manner that we provide any part, free of charge, becoming unfit for use on account of fault in material or workmanship.

INSTRUCTIONS.—Full instructions to every purchaser are given regarding the handling, working, and keeping in order of the Motor and Carriage, and any further information which may at any time be desired will always receive our prompt and best attention.

EXTRA CHARGE FOR RUBBER TYRES.

				£	s.	d
For Carriages to seat Two Persons...	...	...	...	20	0	0
For Carriages to seat Four Persons	...	...	...	25	0	0
For Carriages to seat Six Persons ...	...	...	...	30	0	0
Fancy Awning for Double Carriage ...	...	...	...	6	0	0
„ „ 4-seated Carriage	...	...	...	7	10	0

was first featured in *The Autocar*, as part of the preliminary publicity for the run.

Arrangements were made with Capel, Carless and Leonard to provide fuel supplies at regular intervals for the car (as well as the drivers!), which by now was an open tourer with coachwork built to Sturmey's own design by Mulliners of Northampton. Ashby, a fitter from the Daimler works in Coventry, accompanied the car by train to Wick, losing Sturmey's luggage on the way in Inverness. Friday, October 1st 1897 was a damp day and Sturmey and Ashby elected to remain in Wick before setting out for John O'Groats on the Saturday morning.

"We got away a few minutes after nine for John O'Groats and all the way our progress was like a triumphal procession, the crofters and people in the villages passed lining the road and cheering us. The news of our visit had preceded us so we found all the household in front of the hotel, waving handkerchiefs and welcoming us to John O'Groats."

"We left again at noon, after taking a few photographs and gave the local gamekeeper and his dog a lift for a mile or two..."

Sturmey had written earlier:

"We do not propose in any way to make this a record attempt, as we shall travel purely for pleasure and will not in any way be driving against time."

Sturmey's account gives an initial impression of a leisurely tour down through Scotland and England, with the mileage being built up in easy stages from around thirty up to eighty miles per day. However, at the best of times the journey must have been profoundly uncomfortable for both driver and passenger with frequent stops to deal with mechanical problems, constant bad weather (frequent reference is made to rain, hail and wind) and road conditions which, by any modern standards, were appalling.

A short reference in his diary on October 9th, 1897 gives some indication of the type of roads

The Hon. Evelyn Ellis, pictured here with his daughter after the climb up Malvern Beacon in July 1897. J S Critchley is standing.

JOHN-O'-GROATS TO LAND'S END

Since our last issue we have added some seventy or eighty miles to our score of mileage with our car, last Saturday's run, which was a most successful one, being to Alcester and back, a distance of some fifty-four miles in all. We have now run it, therefore, between three hundred and four hundred miles, and are so satisfied with its running that we have decided on taking a lengthy tour upon it, which will at the same time, we hope, give us a pleasurable holiday, an interesting trip, and prove the all-round capability of the modern autocar. The trip we are proposing is none other than a run from end to end of Great Britain, and by the time this reaches the hands of our readers we shall be well on our way to Wick, wither the car has already preceded us by rail. From Wick, which is the farthest point north the rail reaches, we shall run by car to John-o'-Groats House, the most northerly · point of Scotland, and turning there commence a tour in easy stages, which we propose shall take us to Land's End, the most southerly point of England, and terminate it in London or Coventry. We do not propose in any way to make this a record attempt, as we shall travel purely for pleasure, and will not in any way be driving against time. Fifty to seventy miles per day will, we anticipate, be as much as we shall at any time care to travel. We do not propose to bind ourselves absolutely to any particular route, but, broadly, we propose to follow the cyclists' record route, which is as follows: John-o'-Groat's House, Wick, Dunbeath, Helmsdale, Golspie, Tain, Dingwall, Inverness, Kingussie, Dalwhinnie, Dunkeld, Perth, Kinross, Edinburgh, Biggar, Beattock, Gretna Green, Carlisle, Penrith, Kendal, Lancaster, Preston, Wigan, Warrington, Tarporley, Whitchurch, Wellington, Bridgnorth, Kidderminster, Worcester, Tewkesbury, Gloucester, Bristol, Bridgwater, Taunton, Wellington, Exeter, Launceston, Redruth, and Penzance, to Land's End. For the rest of the journey we shall probably touch at Plymouth, Taunton, Yeovil, Weymouth, Bournemouth, and Stockbridge, as at most of the latter place we shall be visiting friends. If the weather only holds good we are hoping to get a very pleasant trip, and we may possibly meet some of our readers *en route,* who may be interested to see the car. If we have room we may be able occasionally to give a friend a lift, but that will depend on the circumstances. Needless to say, we will keep the readers of *The Autocar* informed as to our weekly progress.

OUR END TO END TRIP

In our last issue we intimated our intention to autocar down from John-o'-Groat's House to Land's End, and we are now fairly *en route.* As we are making copious notes for a full and detailed account of the run for subsequent publication in *The Autocar,* we intend only at present to briefly record our daily progress. We reached Wick by train on Friday evening, and found the car, with Ashby (our engineer) in charge, had arrived by the previous train, but that our baggage had gone astray at Inverness and was not to be found.

The landlord of the Station Hotel was at the train to meet us and very solicitous for our welfare, and already the news of the car's arrival had spread like wildfire, and all the town was agog to see it.

October 2nd.—A fine morning after rain left the roads very wet. We got away a few minutes after nine for John-o'-Groat's, and all the way our progress was like a triumphal procession, the Crofters and people in the villages passed lining the road and cheering us. The news of our visit had preceded us, so we found all the household out in front of the hotel waving handkerchiefs and welcoming us to John-o'Groat's, which we reached in a couple of hours. We left again at noon, after taking a few photographs and gave the local gamekeeper and his dog a lift for a mile or two, and then after a halt to adjust the clutch, which was slipping a bit, and to change one of the lamps, made special progress back to Wick, doing the distance in 1h. 45m., getting in just in time for dinner. As our luggage had not arrived, we were perforce compelled to remain, and perhaps it was as well, for the evening set in wet. Distance for the day, thirty-six miles.

October 3rd.—The weather was very changeable, and soon after we left Wick set in for a good three hours' rain. The road led over the cliffs by the sea, and five or six miles out we rounded a bluff, and ran straight into the wind, which blew with tremendous force, nearly pulled the car up, and carried away our waterproof car cover. The rain hit the face like hail, and we were wet through long ere Latheron was reached. A very bad

descent was negotiated safely, and the big hills, up and down, both here, at Dunbeath, and Berriedale, gave no trouble, although reputed the worst hills on the whole John-o'-Groat's route. Up Berriedale Hill, on the top of the Ord of Caithness — the worst of the three — we stopped for want of oil, and when replenished, the motor was cutting out all the way. We had a lot of trouble after this, which got thoroughly wet and slipped a lot, but doses of resin and some adjustment helped, and we ran down the long inclines of Ord, which are very dangerous owing to the sharp turns, comfortably, and found our missing baggage at the station. The Commercial Hotel was our resting place. Distance for the day, thirty-eight miles.

October 4th.—A glorious morning after the rain. At starting the motor ran poorly, but we got up the two short steep hills out of the town, and then changed the induction valves, which put things right. The road was now fairly level and undulating past Dunrobin Castle to Golspie (vile road through the town) and over the mound. The scenery beautiful. Another big hill, and we ran down to Clashmore Inn for dinner. We readjusted the clutch here, which had been slipping again, and from thence got a glorious run to Bonar Bridge and Tain, through superb scenery and fine fir woods, under which, however, the road was very slippery, and we had to go slow to avoid skidding. There was a market on at Bonar Bridge, and many stoppages had to be made for restive horses, which were met. After this, however, we met but few, and the last twelve miles were done well under the hour. Distance for the day, fifty-seven miles.

October 5th.—This is the best day's run we have had yet. It has been fine, and we have faced a stiff head wind all day. The run of 46½ miles from Tain to Inverness along the coast, over gently undulating roads with splendid surfaces, was made well under four hours, the way being under avenues of beeches and other trees, with beautiful peeps at loch and sea. A cyclist "hung on" to Dingwall, and was very glad of our shelter. From Inverness, however, we got very different driving; the hills were very steep and long, and the roads so rough and heavy on the down grades that it was dangerous to go fast, and the twenty-five miles to Carr Bridge took three and a half hours' steady driving over wild moorland, the motor working grandly all day. Distance for the day, Tain to Carr Bridge, 71½ miles.

OUR END-TO-END TRIP

(Continued from page 655)

October 6th.—We had a brilliant day, and a glorious ride through splendid scenery. From Carr Bridge we rode to Dalwhinnie for lunch, and took on our first supply of petrol (six gallons), and got a scare, as at first it apparently had not come, and we were on our last gallon. Then over the Grampians wild and bleak, with a splendid run down on the other side. No difficulty anywhere. We ran through Blair Athole, and met with a curious adventure which we will relate later on, and then climbed over the beautiful pass of Killiekrankie to Pitlochrie, averaging ten miles an hour all through for the sixty-five miles.

October 7th.—A fine run through Dunkeld, Perth, and Kinross to Burntisland without a stop, except to replenish our oil tanks, and caught the 3.20 ferry boat for Granton, driving the car straight from the quay to the deck of the steamer without gangways. Then we climbed up Pitt Street into Edinburgh, ran up Prince's Street, and gathered an enormous crowd at the Post Office when we called for letters. We ran the sixty-five and a half miles for the day without recharging the water tank, and finished with only half a pint of oil in our tank when we took possession of our fresh supply of eighteen gallons, which the North British Rubber Co. had very kindly taken charge of for us.

October 8th.—We did not get away till after ten, having several calls to make, and then, after giving several influential citizens a ride, we got away with a reader of *The Autocar* as a passenger for Biggar. It was a big climb for several miles, and then it rained heavily, and we had to change our lamps twice. After this, and lunch at Biggar, we had a glorious time, running the forty-seven miles to Lockerbie in four hours, finishing up under a brilliant full moon, and escorted into Lockerbie by a yelling crowd of lunatics. Distance, seventy-six miles for the day.

October 9th.—The run through Gretna Green, across the Border into England, on to Carlisle and Penrith, was a fine one, over splendid roads — the forty-two miles occupying only 3h. 40m. An unattended horse bolted off with a cart just out of Carlisle, but no damage was done. We then dived into the Lake District, forsaking the main road, and running along beautiful

Ullswater, and thence over the Kirkstone Pass to Ambleside. This was the first hill which gave any trouble, as new metal had just been put down on the worst pieces, and we had to walk in places and make three or four halts, but we got up. The descent into Ambleside is particularly dangerous, about 1 in 5 for a mile together, and a narrow winding road. We got down all right, although the brake drum of the footbrake fired half-way down and we had to stop for readjustment and a dose of resin, but we would never attempt such a descent again, it is too dangerous. Distance for the day sixty-six miles.

October 10th was Sunday, and also pouring with rain all day, so we stayed where we were.

October 11th.—Several smart showers were encountered, but we luckily missed a lot of rain which preceded us, though we had heavy roads all day. The climb up from Windermere presented no difficulty, and we ran into Kendal in an hour and a half, where an unattended horse again dashed away with its attached cart, this time going right through the town, though happily doing no damage except to smash off both front wheels. Then on to Lancaster for dinner, and an uneventful run to Preston afterwards, where we called on Messrs. Coulthard's, filled up with petrol, and had a look at their new steam waggon, which seems quite a success. Fifty-seven miles made up the day's total.

October 12th.—Tuesday opened gloriously, a clear sky, a bright sun, and a crisp bracing air. We left Preston at 8.45, and scarcely enjoyed travelling over the vile setts of the Lancashire manufacturing towns of Wigan and Warrington, although some of the intermediate macadam was good, and the scenery in places pretty. Tarporley was our destination for dinner, and we ran out of oil just half a mile short of that place. From thence the Cheshire roads afforded good running, and the excellence of the signposts and milestones testified to the sound work of the Cheshire County Council. A couple of miles short of Whitchurch a halt was made to lubricate the pump, and shortly after leaving that place we took a wrong road, and so made our run to Hodnet about three miles longer than it need have been. Wellington was reached in the dark shortly before seven, and our longest day's ride of eighty-six miles was accomplished in eight hours' running time.

OCTOBER 23RD, 1897

OUR END-TO-END TRIP

(Continued from page 669)

October 13th.—The day opened fine, and we enjoyed a fine run after the colliery district contiguous to Wellington had been passed, running through very pretty country to Bridgnorth. Near the top of Shatterford Hill we had to stop to oil the pump, and numerous delays were caused by restive horses, for several of which we had to stop the motor. After dinner at Worcester we ran on to Kempsey, when a choleric driver of an untamed steed called on the village constable, and took our name and address for driving a locomotive without a red flag in front! The pump required more lubrication, and we changed it at Gloucester, where we ran in, in the wet, about 5.30. Distance for the day, sixty-seven miles.

October 14th was wet, and as we had important business in London (recorded elsewhere) we left the car at Gloucester, returning same night, and being ready on

October 15th to start early. After a showery morning, and very wet and slippery roads, necessitating great care in driving, we ran into Bristol for lunch, and left there in a drenching rain, making for Weston-super-Mare, where we arrived, after traversing very heavy roads, shortly after five, with a score of fifty-seven miles for the day.

October 16th found us favoured with a fine morning after the wet, but the roads were still very slippery, and it was very ticklish driving on the narrow, hogged, rutty roads to East Brent, so that we had to run a speed lower than we should have otherwise done. However, Clarke's Hotel, Taunton, was reached early, and it being market day the car came in for strong (favourable) criticism from the assembled farmers. Eighteen gallons of petrol were taken on board here. A fine run over good roads to Wellington was spoiled by the motor running very poorly, so we halted for thirty-five minutes and ground in the exhaust valves — after 1,100 miles running — after which the motor pulled like an elephant, and we sped along at a great rate for Exeter, just outside of which we met a friend, to whom we gave a lift into the city, the day's journey being sixty-four miles.

October 17th.—Sunday we did not travel. It was, however, a damp and unpleasant day.

J. Henry Sturmey.

October 18th.—On Monday morning we started early to tackle the Devonshire hills. We found no gradients to give us trouble, but the very long ascents made the times slow, although we got some good running on the down grades. Between Okehampton and Launceston a couple of bolts required tightening, which stopped us for a few minutes, and when we reached Launceston the whole town was out to receive us. The run on was over a very wild country with some very trying gradients, but less severe than before, and the last few miles a splendid run down into Bodmin escorted by a crowd of cyclists who had come out to meet us. Here on arrival we found the streets lined with spectators and half a dozen police keeping the road clear for us. Quite a triumphal entry about 5.45. Day's distance, sixty-three miles.

October 19th.—After a dull and misty morning a fine day, and a fine spin over wet roads, but largely perfect surfaces to Redruth, the long steep hill down through the centre of the town requiring great care. A wild country of used and disused mines brought us quickly to Camborne, where, as at Redruth, crowds were awaiting our arrival. After lunch we took a friend resident there on board, and sped off over magnificent roads to Hayle and Penzance, making good time. Here we were met by an advance guard of cyclists, and the whole population had turned out to receive us, with the police keeping the route, the crowd cheering and waving hats and handkerchiefs as we drove steadily up the steep hill into the town to the hotel, where we put down our friend, and after a short stay proceeded. The next five miles were very bad indeed, both as to surface and gradient, and after another five miles of passable, though varying road,

Land's End Hotel

hove in sight, and by 4.35 our drive from end to end of Great Britain was pleasantly, successfully, and satisfactorily completed without a single breakdown, the entire distance travelled being 929 miles, accomplished in 93½ hours running time, or an average from end to end of within a few yards of ten miles per hour. The motor is pulling better than when we started, and the car apparently but little the worse for the journey.

It is now our intention to travel leisurely home, visiting friends *en route*, and most probably touching at Plymouth, Exeter, Taunton, Yeovil, Weymouth, Poole, Bournemouth, Southampton, Winchester, and probably London, which will bring the tour up to between 1,200 and 1,300 miles. Up to the present we have since September 9th, when we received it, driven our car just 1,273 miles.

The first motor car (Coventry-built Daimler), ever to accomplish the journey from John O'Groats to Land's End.

involved. Sturmey and Ashby had reached Kirkstone pass and were descending into Amberside:

> "We got down all right although the brake drums of the footbrake failed halfway down and we had to stop for re-adjustment and a dose of resin, but we would never attempt such a descent again, it is too dangerous!"

Few of the spectators had seen a motor vehicle and specially printed cards were handed out en-route:

What is it?
It is an Autocar,
Some people call it a motor car,
It is worked by petroleum motor,
The motor is of four horsepower,
It will run sixty miles on one change of oil,
No, it can't explode, there is no boiler,
It can travel at fourteen miles per hour,
Ten to eleven is the average pace,
It can be started in two minutes,
There are eight ways of stopping it so it can't run away,

It is steered with one hand,
Speed is mainly controlled by the foot,
It can be stopped in ten feet when travelling at full speed,
It carries four gallons of oil and sixteen gallons of water,
The water is to keep the engine cool,
It costs less than ¾ penny a mile to run ,
The car can carry four people,
It can get up any ordinary hill,
It was built by the Daimler Motor Company in Coventry and cost £370,
We have come from John O'Groat's house,
We are going to Land's End,
We are not record-breaking but touring for pleasure.

By the time Sturmey's journey was finished, he had covered nearly 1600 miles (not 1400 as he estimated in his account). Bearing in mind the road and weather conditions, the journey was a remarkable achievement by the standards of the time. There can be little doubt that it provided much favourable publicity for the motor car when it was regarded by many with almost superstitious dread.

A short break in the journey allowed Sturmey to

attend the first Annual General Meeting of the Daimler Company on 14th October 1897. This was an optimistic affair. Lawson had resigned to pursue other interests in the Great Horseless Carriage Company, but Sturmey was able to persuade other shareholders that all was going to plan. Tributes were paid to the reliability of the new Daimlers by those owners present and the accounts showed healthy profits and a sizeable balance at the bank.

Unfortunately, this was little more than window-dressing. Underneath an over-optimistic exterior lay serious management problems. One of the most pressing difficulties lay in the day-to-day management of the Company. For a start, all members of the Board of Directors were but part-timers with no one director dedicated to the full-time administration of the Company. This resulted in poor management and what little time the Board was able to dedicate to the business being used for destructive in-fighting which was to feature in the Company's fortunes for the next year.

The demonstration given to the Prince of Wales in 1896 was followed by a further demonstration in June 1898. Continuing the association with the Prince, whose interest had continued since the first demonstration, the Daimler Company arranged for five cars to be placed at the Prince's disposal at Warwick Castle. Three were of the standard type

with twin-cylinder 4HP engines, tiller steering and solid tyres, a fourth was powered by a four-cylinder engine and the fifth was the vehicle used by Henry Sturmey on the John 'O Groats to Lands End run. Despite minor mechanical mishaps, the Prince was impressed by the demonstration and had his first trip on the public highway in a motor car.

Sturmey, who had presided as Chairman since Lawson's resignation, continued to attract some severe criticism from management and Daimler shareholders, culminating in a motion to have him replaced by Richard Bannister in July 1898. Bannister, a barrister, had no connection with the motor industry and no engineering expertise. Unfortunately his appointment did little to help matters and an extraordinary general meeting of the shareholders of the Company was convened for 8th August 1898 to deal with allegations made by Sturmey about the Board's conduct.

The meeting was stormy to say the least, and a "full and frank discussion" ensued, with the meeting finally resolving to form a shareholder's committee to investigate Sturmey's own charges against his fellow directors. This committee met throughout the months from August to December of 1898 and on December 10th it reported its findings to the remainder of the shareholders.

These were hardly surprising, given the amount

Claimed to be a week's typical output from the Coventry Daimler works. In fact, the early Daimlers took up to three months to assemble. One reason was that the engine components were not made to sufficiently fine tolerances to allow "production line" assembly. Parts were produced in small batches where the quality control was marginal and many major components required extensive finishing just to fit. Bodies were individually hand-built and fitted.

of dirty linen so far washed in public! The committee had concluded that the original prospectus had been misleading, there had been no proper control of the business, a payment of £40,000 to Lawson's syndicate had been excessive if not bordering on fraudulent, directors' fees and perks had been excessive and the accounts presented at the first Annual General Meeting in 1897 had been misleading. The committee recommended that the Company be wound up, reconstructed with adequate working capital and that a paid managing director be appointed with a substantial interest in the Company's fortunes. This report had the galvanizing effect of uniting the Board, if only to answer the allegations made against it.

A second Annual General Meeting was held on 7th January 1899. On the agenda was the committee's report on the Company and the resolution to wind up the Company. By this time both Gottlieb Daimler and J A Bradshaw had resigned and the Honorable Evelyn Ellis and William Wright had retired by rotation and did not wish to be re-elected as directors. F R Simms had resigned

as consulting engineer in 1897 and the value of the shares had fallen since the last meeting.

For three and a half hours the heated arguments ensued. Finally, a shareholder managed to move a resolution of confidence in the Board. This was narrowly passed and E H Bayley and Sir Edward Jenkinson were elected to fill two of several vacancies.

The new Board found themselves faced with an administrative mess. Bayley and Jenkinson lost no time in dismissing the entire London-based clerical staff and 64% of the production staff in Coventry. The chaotic and inefficient book-keeping system was overhauled and a new management team was recruited. By the end of 1899, these measures had begun to take effect.

A third Annual General Meeting was held on 18th December 1899. Despite Daimler vehicles enjoying success in public trials and tests, a combination of bad luck and bad management had resulted in some exceedingly bad publicity.

The first ever fatal motor accident had taken place on 25th February 1899 at the bottom of a steep

A group of Daimler shareholders at the Coventry factory in 1897.

Street scene featuring several early Daimlers, circa 1898.

winding hill in Harrow. The vehicle, a Daimler Wagonette on a demonstration trip from London, had descended Grove Hill at speed and on attempting a sharp turn, the driver, Edwin Sewell, had lost control when the wooden spokes of one of the back wheels had collapsed. The six occupants of the Wagonette were thrown into the road. Sewell was killed and one of the passengers, a Major Richer, died later as a result of the injuries sustained in his fall.

Henry Sturmey wrote an ill-timed and ill-informed article in *The Autocar* blaming Sewell, an employee, for the accident. Being a then director of the Company, this was tantamount to admitting that the Company was responsible and it was later forced to settle actions instituted by the injured parties. Notwithstanding the bad publicity from this, which later resulted in the local authority imposing a 5mph

speed limit, it was found that Company vehicles were not insured against road risks. Claims and costs were therefore met out of shareholders funds.

A second accident, this time involving a collision between two vehicles, resulted in further settlements being made out of shareholders funds. Incredibly, Sturmey had again commented on the matter in *The Autocar*! His resignation in May 1899 must have come as a relief to his fellow directors.

Where the directors attentions were concentrated on the manufacture of motor vehicles some modest success was achieved, with an operating profit of £1,000. Wrongdoings and incompetence were blamed on the old Board of Directors and were stressed as the reason for shareholders not receiving dividends but the in-fighting, which had been a characteristic of the Company over the last two years, had ceased for the time being.

Daimler Wagonette, circa 1900.

Daimler shareholders, this time pictured in 1900.

Bristol's first Daimler Charabanc trip in 1898. The outing was organised by Mr A E Johnson of the Bristol Motor Company. He is at the tiller of the left-hand Daimler. The cars had rear water tanks that frequently boiled over, tiller steering, and were lit by candles in carriage lamps. The claimed maximum speed was 14mph and it was said that the cars could stop in ten feet. This is probably exaggerated, as Henry Sturmey testifies of brake failure in his account of the 1897 End-to-End run

5. THE LANCHESTER ENGINE COMPANY

"He (Gibson) told me that undoubtedly the Receivership had been a great blunder, and the Chairman and Directors had to save face, otherwise they would have been the laughing stock of Birmingham for not supporting a prosperous business."

Frederick Lanchester, 1938.

The Lanchester Engine Company Limited was first registered on 13th December 1899. The first directors were: Charles Vernon Pugh (Chairman), John V Pugh, Hamilton Barnsley, J S Taylor and James Whitfield.

Frederick Lanchester was appointed general manager of the Company and Frank Lanchester appointed company secretary.

Of the above, only the Lanchester brothers had been members of the original syndicate. The Pugh group had joined just prior to the formation of the Company. From an authorised capital of £60,000 only £45,525 was allotted, with only £25,000 cash being available as working capital. The remainder was represented by the Lanchester patents and the assets of the original syndicate.

Writing in 1938, Frederick Lanchester had his reservations about this. His original arrangement with Whitfields had been for a 50/50 split of the financing of the development of the cars.

> *"In view of the original arrangement, my contribution as patentee, which included not only the original patents, but all the improvements related to motor vehicles, was represented by a modest £1,000 vis-a-vis the other members of the syndicate"*

He regarded this as a gross undervaluation of his work, carried out without remuneration over the previous five years. Bearing in mind that a value of £500,000 had been put on the Daimler patents by Lawson in 1896, this was quite understandable. Investors had been given little to inspire faith in such a venture. Lawson's sharp practice, together with adverse publicity relating to Daimler, amongst others, made a new motor manufacturing concern seem a risky venture to a cautious investor. Once the Armourer Mills factory in Sparkbrook, Birmingham had been altered and equipped, there was very little of the £25,000 cash left. Frederick Lanchester later remarked:

> *"I well knew that the finance would not prove sufficient for the undertaking.... (but) the provision of money I did not consider to be my job: as General Manager, having obtained the sanction of the Board for a programme, any (of my) responsibility was limited to carrying it out"*

The work of altering the new factory carried on through most of 1900. Frederick Lanchester was by nature a perfectionist and was not prepared to commence production until he could do so on the basis of precision-made interchangeable parts. As there was no technology which could be drawn on in 1900, most tasks had to be reduced to first principles. The directors frequently exhorted Lanchester to commence production of anything so at least they had something to sell! George Lanchester recalled in 1948:

> *"Looking back, our policy may be criticized as extravagant, but had we failed to adopt the ideal of accuracy, I do not believe that our cars would have achieved the reputation for quality which they earned, and which has been fully justified."*

In this refusal to proceed as directed, albeit for very sound engineering reasons, the beginnings of Frederick Lanchesters' conflicts with his Board of Directors for the whole of the period of his involvement with the company can be traced. Orders for the vehicles were not encouraging, although Frank and George Lanchester did what they could by advertising and demonstrating the new cars at every opportunity, there were insufficient funds for a sustained sales campaign, which resulted in few customers and severe cash-flow problems.

The Company's reputation was not helped by the performance of its two entrants in the 1000 Miles Trial organised by the Automobile Club of Great Britain and Ireland. The importance of this trial at the time cannot be underestimated. The Automobile Club realised that solid achievement rather than mere spectacle was required if the motor car was ever to become widely accepted by the British public. The very title was a challenge to the motor industry and to the imagination. At that time the car that ran twenty miles without breakdowns was regarded as something of a curiosity. The covering of a

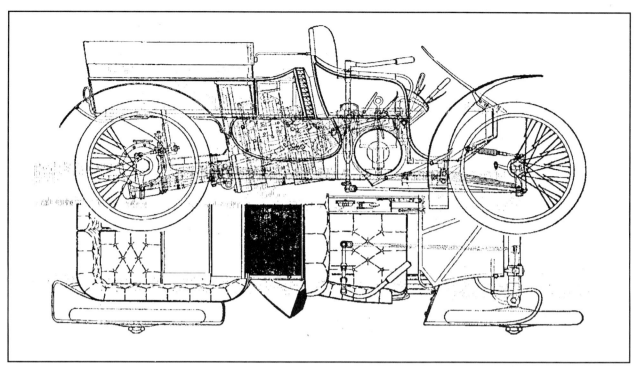

Drawings of the first 10HP Lanchester production model of 1900-1901.

Experimental car of 1903, featuring water-cooled, rather than the more common Lanchester air-cooled, engine.

1904 Lanchester four-cylinder 12HP car now preserved by the British Motor Industry Heritage Trust.

distance of one thousand miles was therefore considered to be an impossibility. Supported by Alfred Harmsworth (later Lord Northcliffe), proprietor of the *Daily Mail*, organiser Claude Johnson canvassed the press, and personally travelled the proposed course and cleared the trial with each of the constabularies through which the trial vehicles would be passing.

This preparation was clearly very important, since officials needed some comfort that this was a serious trial and not merely a continental-style road race. In addition, publicity along the route would be generated by the holding of a small exhibition in each of Bristol, Cheltenham, Birmingham, Manchester, Kendal, Carlisle, Edinburgh, Newcastle-upon-Tyne, York, Leeds, Bradford, Sheffield, Lincoln,

Nottingham and London with a one-week speed trial at Welbeck Park. Although the final itinerary varied slightly from the original plan, the trial was widely thought to have been an unqualified success and provided much sought-after publicity for the successful entrants. Of the 65 cars entered, 35 completed the trial.

Unfortunately, both Lanchester entrants were forced to withdraw early on in the trial with mechanical problems. By contrast, all thirteen of the Daimler entrants completed the course.

Anthony Bird and Francis Hutton-Stott in the book, *Lanchester Motor Cars*, went to considerable pains to point out that where the Lanchester cars did perform, they did so extremely well. The maximum speed of 30mph available to George Lanchester and

Advertisement for the Lanchester Engine Company, shortly after the order from the War Office for a batch of ten Lanchester cars. George Lanchester is seated to the left in the rear passenger compartment, together with Archie Millership, the firms Chief Tester and Demonstrator, described by Lanchester as a "wizard at skidding". Millership was a key figure in the early Lanchester Company, second only to the Lanchester brothers themselves.

Archie Millership had been (they said) used to good advantage throughout. However, at the time, the damage to the reputation of the cars was done by their failure to finish the trial, which was compounded by writers who simply did not comprehend the engineering principles behind features such as air-cooled engines, which were contrary to accepted practice at the time, though commonplace now. At a time when this sort of technology was beyond the understanding of the man on the Clapham omnibus, considerable damage could be done by a self-appointed expert writing in the press.

Undeterred by such setbacks, the Company went ahead with production, and by August 1901 the Lanchester 10HP air-cooled production cars were on the road. Production was organised on a planned interchangeable parts system with tolerances and gauge limits specified to pre-determined standards. The 10HP model proved to be a modest success and in 1902, a water-cooled 12HP model was introduced. Capable of up to 40mph, three to four hundred were sold at a price of £525-£550. 16HP and 18HP models followed in 1903 and a four-cylinder 20HP model, capable of 50mph, was introduced in 1904. Cantilever springing had by now been developed which together with the rigid chassis and body construction gave a very comfortable ride.

A 16HP air-cooled model, driven by C W Dixon and Archie Millership, the firm's chief tester and demonstrator, completed a trial of 500 miles in 1903, averaging 22mph at 19.8 miles per gallon.

Ten years later when Dixon repeated the run in the same car (this time with water-cooling), the average speed rose to 24mph and fuel consumption improved to 28.3 miles per gallon.

Despite making a healthy profit of £8,669 in 1903, the Company was beginning to suffer from the effects of overtrading. Although business was brisk, the profit was insufficient to attract new investors. Unfortunately, investment was vital for the continued well-being of the business. An attempt to raise a further £24,000 by public subscription failed, not least because the directors had insufficient faith to take up any of the offered shares themselves. On 4 March 1904, the Lanchester Engine Company was found to be insolvent and was put into Receivership by its creditors, to whom the sum of £20,000 was owing. It is indeed doubtful if this Receivership was ever necessary.

The Company made respectable profits even from the beginning of the Receivership and, indeed, continued to do so afterwards. Creditors had clearly been impatient and hasty in their actions, which resulted in humiliation for the directors, whose poor management was found to have starved the company of working capital. The reconstruction of the business resulted in the formation of *The Lanchester Motor Company Limited*, which was forced on a reluctant Board of Directors who accepted it grudgingly in order to save face. Once this painful process was over, the Lanchester car, at least for the time being, still had a future.

6. SILENT KNIGHTS, SMALL ARMS AND THE GREAT WAR

"It seems to me that the Daimler people are running this war"

> The Prince of Wales (later King Edward VIII)
> on visiting the front

"Frank made it his duty to maintain close touch with the services, and after much persistence on his part, the Ministries discovered our greatest contribution to the war effort lay in our own trade...not in ruining our plant by producing shells!"

> George Lanchester, 1948.

Compared with previous meetings, the 1900 Annual General Meeting of the Daimler Motor Company Limited was a quiet affair. A profit of £4,430 had been made and steps were being taken to cope with new orders and the expansion of the business. This had been helped by the placing of an order by the Prince of Wales (later King Edward VII) for a Daimler 6HP, which had been delivered to the Royal household in March. With this optimistic outlook the future was indeed rosy, so much so that the eagle eye of the first chairman and promoter once again had focused on the Company.

Harry J Lawson made his takeover bid during 1900, offering £60,000 in cash to the shareholders together with £50,000 in preference shares, an eleven for ten offer. On the face of it, this may well have been an acceptable offer, but the Board were wary of Lawson and had insisted on him depositing a bond of £10,000 in cash to be forfeit if the offer failed to go through. Lawson lost his nerve and withdrew the offer. After the initial hubbub over his offer had died down, a new Board was elected, chaired by Sir Edward Jenkinson.

Lawson was to withdraw from the motor industry after this. A series of failed lawsuits in 1900 and 1901 for claims relating to patents bought so extravagantly in the 1890s was followed by an indictment in 1904 on conspiracy to defraud. Later sentenced to one year's hard labour for making false statements to induce persons to buy shares or lend money, Lawson then confined himself to writing in the motoring press. In 1925, his fortune reduced to just £99, he died. The Daimler name is the only survivor of Lawson's many speculations.

Meanwhile at Daimler, the Company was beginning to run into further problems. The root cause was lack of management resource and working capital. Insolvency was narrowly avoided thanks to the Hon. Evlyn Ellis, who had subscribed £13,000 of his personal fortune to keep the Company afloat. A debenture issue in 1901 proved to be a failure and the Company recorded a loss for that year. By 1902 a modest profit of £1,200 had been achieved, but only at the cost of exhausting cash resources to introduce a new model range and to modernise the factory. This unsatisfactory situation continued into 1903.

There was no difficulty in selling cars. The problem was that there was no stock. There was no stock because the Company had insufficient money to pay for components and the wages of the men needed to assemble them into finished motor cars. With no stock available, delivery times increased, inconveniencing the customers who then went and bought the more readily available imported foreign models. The Company made a healthy paper profit, but lived from hand to mouth so that a fire in April 1903, which destroyed the paint shop and only seven cars, was to put back production for a whole year. In addition, the Company relied on only two basic models.

At this point, it is worth drawing a comparison between the Daimler and Lanchester companies. Both had potential for making considerable profit, with a growing public demand for their cars. Competition was fierce and both needed to expand to compete with foreign manufacturers who were able to operate with more than adequate finance. This was in direct contrast to both the English companies, who had to rely on substantial deposits from customers to pay the wage bills of the workmen who assembled their cars. Both companies laboured under the dual handicap of poor management and under-capitalisation. The way in which these problems were tackled explains why Daimler was able to achieve pre-eminence, despite the technical genius behind the Lanchester vehicles.

On December 8th 1904, after months of careful

Proof 16. 17/2/1902.

The Subscription List will open on the   day of February, 1902, and will
close on or before the following   day of February, 1902.

THE
DAIMLER MOTOR COMPANY,
LIMITED.

(Incorporated under the Companies' Acts, 1862-1890.)

CAPITAL - - £100,000.
DIVIDED INTO—

100,000 Ordinary Shares of £1 each, all of which (except 370 Shares forfeited) have
been issued and are fully paid up.

ISSUE OF
£60,000 Five per Cent. First Mortgage Debenture Stock at par,

The **Debenture Stock and the Interest thereon will be secured by a Trust Deed and by a
Mortgage on the Leasehold property of the Company, and will be a floating charge on all the Assets
of the Company,** and will be redeemable at the option of the Company at any time after the 28th day of
February, 1917, **at the rate of £105 for every £100 of Stock,** subject to six months previous notice, and
in case the Company shall go into voluntary liquidation for the purpose of reconstruction, amalgamation, or
for any other purpose, the Stock will be redeemable at a rate not less than £105 for every £100 of Stock.

The Trust Deed will contain a covenant by the Company to pay to the Trustees upon the 28th
day of February, 1905, and on each succeeding 28th day of February, until the whole of the Stock is
redeemed, the sum of £2,500 as a Sinking Fund for the redemption of the said Debenture Stock, or at the
option of the Company they may transfer to the Trustees Debenture Stock of this issue of the same par value in
lieu of such cash payment, or may make up the sum partly in cash and partly in such Debenture Stock.

The Trust Deed provides that the Company shall have the right to purchase the issued Stock at any
time on the open market at a price not exceeding the redemption price.

Interest will be payable half-yearly on the 1st day of January, and the 1st day of July, in each year.

The Stock will be transferable in multiples of £1.

**Applications for the above-mentioned First Mortgage Debenture Stock, at par, will be received
by THE LONDON, CITY AND MIDLAND BANK, LIMITED, payable as follows :—**

10% on Application,
40% on Allotment,
50% one Month after Allotment.

The first payment of interest calculated from the dates of actual payment of the various instalments,
will be made on the 1st day of July next.

The whole amount of subscription may at any time after allotment be paid up in full, and the amount
thereof will carry full interest from the day of such payment.

Trustees for Debenture Stockholders.
The Honble. GEORGE EDWYN HILL-TREVOR, 14, Onslow Square, S.W.
The Honble. HAROLD P. MOSTYN, The White House, Chelsea, S.W.

Solicitors to the Trustees.
Messrs. CUTLER, ALLINGHAM & NESFIELD, 15, Duke Street, St. James', S.W.

Directors.
Sir EDWARD G. JENKINSON, K.C.B., *Chairman.*
E. MANVILLE, Esq. (of the Firm of Kincaid, Waller & Manville, Electrical Engineers,
Westminster).
Captain C. C. LONGRIDGE, R.A., M.I.M.E.

Bankers.
THE LONDON, CITY & MIDLAND BANK, Coventry; 5, Threadneedle Street, London, E.C., and Branches.

Solicitors to the Company.
Messrs. GREENIP, SNELL & CO., 1 & 2, George Street, Mansion House, E.C.

Auditors.
Messrs. MONKHOUSE, STONEHAM & CO., Chartered Accountants, 28 & 29, St. Swithin's Lane, E.C.

Brokers.
LONDON : Messrs. JOHN GIBBS, SON & CO., 29, Cornhill, E.C., and Stock Exchange.
BIRMINGHAM : Messrs. H. & H. FITTER & CO., Paradise Street, and Stock Exchange.
MANCHESTER :

Secretary and Registered Offices.
G. T. GRANT, Daimler Works, Coventry.

The prospectus issued for the five per cent debenture issue of 1902

Prospectus for the 1902 debenture issue. This proved to be a failure and the Company underwent a major reconstruction
two years later.

40

Royal Patronage:
August 1899. The Prince of Wales (later King Edward VII), seated in a 12HP Daimler Wagonette with John Scott-Montagu. The first order was placed by the Royal Household in 1900. The British Royal family continues to use Daimlers into the 1990s.

Pictured here is a particularly fine Daimler, delivered to the Royal Mews in 1904.

planning by a far-sighted Board of Directors, the Daimler Motor Company Limited resolved to transfer it's assets to a new company, *The Daimler Motor Company (1904) Limited* and then go into voluntary liquidation. Worthless assets were to be written off and the shareholders were asked to subscribe additional working capital, which they duly did. In 1905, additional shares were issued and for the first time the shareholders received a dividend.

In the meantime the Company continued to be active in extending its premises. In 1905, a reconstruction programme commenced which resulted in new machine and erecting shops and the major refurbishment of a four storey building acquired upon the liquidation of the Motor Manufacturing Company. The provision of these premises ensured that by 1913, the workforce of 5,000 could be safely accommodated, Daimler being one of the largest single employers in the engineering industry in Coventry, by that time.

If the years up to 1904 were of continuing uncertainty, the following years saw the fortunes of both the Daimler and Lanchester companies improve. Under Sir Edward Jenkinson as Chairman until 1906 and beyond, when he was eventually succeeded by Percy Martin, The Daimler Motor Company (1904) Limited was placed on the path to prosperity, with increasing sales, Royal patronage and financial stability. However, this was not without some significant operational problems.

On 13th February 1906 *The Motor* reported that "All the motor car manufacturers in Coventry are extremely busy, and many of the works are running overtime." Daimler was no exception to this and prospered that year recording a substantial profit of £185,785. Increased competition however, resulted in a price cutting policy throughout the industry, which forced Daimler to cut the prices of its 1907 cars by some £200. This benefited the customer, but then placed the Company in the position of having to satisfy increasing demand. On 5th April 1910 *The Motor* again commented on this aspect of the operation noting that "well over 3,000 men are working day and night without a stop".

With increasing production, one of the major headaches facing the Company was quality control. The reliability and build quality of Daimler vehicles was, together with Royal patronage, absolutely essential to its reputation. Whilst Lanchester Cars had quality control built into the manufacturing process, Daimler became dependent on component suppliers. In 1902, a laboratory had been constructed for the purpose of testing supplied materials, which in 1903 discovered that the engine valves were defective and resulted in manufacture being commissioned in-house.

Concern over quality resulted in significant investments in ailing firms such as Coventry Chain, which received £30,000 of funding from Daimler who preferred to make the outlay rather than see a

A 1905 Daimler delivered to a Mr Pochin of Leicestershire.

quality component manufacturer go under. This ensured that the Company had a reliable supply of nuts and bolts, an essential ingredient to the build quality of the Daimler vehicles.

Components was one matter, but it was entirely another problem to ensure that the work force could assemble them into the finished product. Numerous problems arose when trying to deal with an increasingly sophisticated and unionised workforce. This was particularly apparent when management attempted to improve productivity through the manipulation of working conditions and methods of reward. The introduction of piecework rates and the system of payment known as premium bonus, where a job was timed and a bonus paid on the basis of time saved was fiercely attacked by the unions, who claimed that the system was excessively biased to the employers' interest, with little benefit accruing to employee.

Daimler was continually attacked by the unions as a result of this system, with the Company's tinsmiths striking in 1907 over the introduction of the system, which resulted in the original arrangement being reinstated after seven weeks. Shopfloor unrest continued through 1908, with allegations of incompetent rate-fixing, arbitrary reductions in the times allocated to tasks and non-payment of bonuses, a particularly contentious point, as many employees did not receive bonuses until several months after jobs were completed.

Although pressure on the workforce was one means of increasing profitability, the increasing use of machine tools certainly contributed to the reduction in costs per unit of some 15% during 1904-1906. Though not without its problems, this improvement was to the credit of Percy Martin, who had experience of production methods in the United States and Continental Europe prior to his move to Daimler. As the Company's then second largest shareholder, he had a more than adequate incentive to ensure its long term prosperity.

The Daimler sleeve-valve engine was widely used in commercial and public utility vehicles. The vehicle pictured below is a 1910 KPL omnibus.

Daimler Commercial Vehicles:
Daimler built a variety of commercial vehicles which were utilised by the Fire Service and numerous different firms.
The fire engine is a works vehicle at Daimler's Radford Plant and the firemen are Daimler employees. The trucks
were part of a fleet used by BP to distribute petrol, and the van carried baby food.

The Lanchester Company also prospered, ironically after being placed in the hands of a Receiver. Frederick Lanchester recalled that shortly after the appointment of A H Gibson as Receiver on March 4th 1904:

"Gibson, after running the business for a couple of months found he was making steady profits and I do not believe at any time during the Receivership did the Company cease to make profits."

In fact, the Company's fortunes turned and it continued to be profitable until 1915. However, this was at some personal cost to Lanchester himself, who had to relinquish the post of General Manager and had his salary reduced from £350 per annum to £250 per annum. He also found himself a scapegoat for the directors' lack of foresight in failing to adequately finance the business. Lanchester's involvement in the management of the business diminished, though he himself regarded it as an opportunity to pursue other interests:

"...the work I was called on to do did not average a quarter of what I had done previously - about ten to twelve hours per day - so that, in measure of time, £250 per annum was a princely salary. I found myself at liberty to resume my work on aerodynamics and aviation...I became attached to the Daimler Company as Consultant and Technical Advisor... the Institute of Automobile Engineers was formed and from the first I took a prominent part being elected President for the years 1910-1911."

Following the Receivership a cheap light car was suggested but the Company did not develop the idea, preferring to take on the Birmingham selling agency for the American-built Oldsmobile, which was probably intended to assist cash-flow in this difficult period. By the 1909 season, the tiller steering which characterised Lanchester cars was replaced with the more conventional steering wheel, although the tiller remained an option for those that preferred it until 1911, when Lanchester began to adopt more conventional technology.

The operation of the early Lanchester cars was idiosyncratic, which goes some way to explaining the initial customer resistance to them. However, compared with their contemporary competitors they were better engineered, quieter and smoother in their operation. Whilst the modern arrangement for accelerator pedal, brake and clutch was coming into use elsewhere, on Lanchesters only the left foot was engaged on the throttle. The right foot was idle, the right hand was for control of the "side steering lever" (tiller) and the left hand dealt with the rest. A trigger operated the three gears, which could be pre-selected to "low", "intermediate" or "high" which engaged indirect forward gears and reverse as well as acting as an auxiliary brake. Additional levers served the hand petrol pump, the two governors and the vapour regulator for the wick carburettor.

From 1895 to 1909 Frederick Lanchester had been solely responsible for every aspect of the Lanchester car's design, down to the smallest detail, with brother George acting as right-hand man in the execution of these designs. In 1910-11 the roles began to reverse with the introduction of the 25HP and 38HP cars, which conformed to more conventional motoring design practice, utilising a steering wheel rather than a tiller and a foot operated clutch for the first time.

By 1913, George Lanchester realised that despite a number of technical advantages in the unorthodox Lanchester designs, there was need to design a car of conventional appearance utilising a conventional side-valve engine.

In this he was influenced by the non-technical Board of Directors. The result, the Lanchester "Sporting Forty" was a moderate success with motoring journalists, but disliked by the designer.

The London depot of the Lanchester Company at 95 New Bond Street. Pictured in the foreground is a 1910 Lanchester 25HP.

These two pictures demonstrate the radical difference between the styling of the vehicles designed by Frederick and George Lanchester. The first is the bonnetless design by Frederick Lanchester from around 1910. Below is the Lanchester Sporting Forty designed by George Lanchester. Less than five years seperates the two cars.

Charles T Knight was an American journalist from Wisconsin, who, while campaigning on behalf of agricultural interests who wished to impose tax on margarine, had become passionately interested in motor cars. In 1901, when the majority of cars were noisy, smelly bone-shakers Knight sought to find a solution to the noise problem. Knight could not abide noise and was particularly unimpressed by the development of six-cylinder poppet-valve engines, describing this in 1908 as "continuity of noise, which they call silence!"

The development of a silent-running internal combustion engine became an obsession with Knight, who although a complete amateur, had studied every written work and patent in the hope of solving the problem. A lateral thinker, he abandoned any attempt to improve conventional designs and constructed an engine using sliding cast-iron liners. Encouraged by early successes, by spring 1905 he had abandoned journalism and had his first car on the road. The car was brought to England in 1906, and after a number of modifications by Frederick Lanchester, who was now working for

Daimler as a consultant, the "Silent Knight" double sleeve-valve engine was put into production in 1909.

The "Silent Knight" met with immediate hostility from every quarter. The resulting publicity was not a good advertisement for the Company still emerging from the financial doldrums of earlier years and the Board acted quickly in commissioning the RAC to submit two engines to the most stringent tests then available.

An official challenge was issued by the Company to its rivals. Any manufacturer of poppet-valve engines which within three months from 4th April 1909 obtained RAC certificates exceeding in merit those obtained by the Daimler Company for its sleeve-valve engines would receive a cheque for £250 deposited by the Company for that purpose. There were no takers.

Not only were there changes in technology , but also changes in management. Oddly enough, the key figure was also an American, Percy Martin. Born in Colombia, Ohio in 1871, Martin graduated as a mechanical engineer in 1892. His involvement with Daimler arose from an accidental meeting with a

1909 Daimler sleeve-valve Drophead Coupe. This vehicle is still in regular use in Australia.

Racing Daimlers:
Many pioneering motor manufacturers made a practice of participating in trials and races as a means of getting publicity and field testing new cars. Daimler was no exception to this, although its racing achievements were mostly confined to the years leading up to the First World War. Awards were gained at the Shelsley Walsh hillclimb in 1905 by E M C Instone in a 35HP Daimler, and Daimler cars featured in the last of the Gordon Bennett Races. By 1907, the emphasis had switched from speed trials and hillclimbs to distance and endurance tests.

The above car featured in the Targa Florio in 1907, a tortuous three-lap race over the Great Madione circuit in Sicily. Each lap was over ninety miles long and only thirty out of the forty starters completed the course. George Ison, Daimler's works tester, managed to beat the 1905 winning time by over half-an-hour, but was hampered by problems with the car's clutch and lost speed in the second two laps, finishing 13th overall.

Mr H F L Orcutt, who was recruiting a works manager following the departure of J S Critchley. Martin joined the Company in 1901 staying until his retirement in 1934. By 1906, he had been promoted to the position of Managing Director, recruiting a fellow-director, Edward Manville and encouraging the development of Knight's engine.

The sleeve-valve "Silent Knight" provided Daimler with much needed commercial success. 1908 had been a bad year for the Company with losses amounting to £49,286. Poor production and poor trading conditions were the reasons cited. By the end of 1909, the loss had been reversed, and by 1910 profits exceeded £100,000. The Company had become a leading motor manufacturer and began to attract the attention of a much larger group

which was seeking to expand its own motor manufacturing base.

The Birmingham Small Arms Company had developed over a period of 150 years, originating in 1689, following the granting of a government contract to five Birmingham gunsmiths to supply two hundred muskets per month "at seventeen shillings per piece ready money". Fourteen gunsmiths later formed into the Birmingham Small Arms Trade, which later incorporated itself into *The Birmingham Small Arms Company* ("BSA") in 1861. Until 1879, the Company prospered, but the prolonged peace in Europe lessened the demand for its principal product and it was forced to diversify.

The manufacture of cycles began in 1881, and

the Company enjoyed considerable success on the back of the popular cycling movement which grew at the same time. An upsurge in demand for rifles halted the manufacture of complete cycles until 1908, although the Company did continue to manufacture components. In 1909 BSA introduced their first motor cycle. Although the Company had manufactured cars since 1907, the directors concluded that only a substantial acquisition would gain them entry to the then lucrative motor trade.

A concern was found which was capable of generating good profits, but which had a low share price. The market capitalisation (ie - the value of all the issued shares at current prices), of the target company was low compared to the value of the assets and there was valuable goodwill attached to its name, *The Daimler Motor Co. (1904) Limited.*

The architect of this scheme was Dudley Docker. Born in 1852 in Smethwick, Docker was the son of a prominent Birmingham solicitor. A prodigious businessman, Docker acquired his reputation in 1902 when he managed the merger of five of the major rolling stock companies into the *Metropolitan Amalgamated Carriage and Wagon Company,* widely regarded as having transformed Britain's industrial infrastructure. By 1906 he had been invited to join the Board of BSA, becoming BSA's deputy chairman. BSA's motor division had failed under E E Bageley, described by Docker as:

> *"incapable of organisation, his only solution for bottlenecks being to employ more staff; he had presided over anarchy not only in design, production and after-sales service, but in simple matters like stock-taking and the supply of cars".*

A Daimler owner since 1906, Docker was acquainted with Daimler's top management, Percy Martin and Edward Manville. A deal was eventually struck whereby BSA would pay £600,000 for Daimler.

On September 2nd 1910, *The Financial Times* reported that "negotiations were proceeding for an amalgamation of the BSA and the Daimler Motor Co. Limited". This amalgamation was described as "the most important ever effected in the motor industry" on September 27th.

The proposed terms were put to an independent consultant with considerable experience in the financial affairs of the motor industry, Mr A H Gibson, formerly Receiver of the Lanchester Engine

Daimlers workshop at Coventry, circa 1912. Tourers, limousines and commercial vehicles can be seen clearly.

Daimler Charabancs were a popular feature of English life prior to and following the First World War. Primarily used for excursions and holiday trips, they provided a cheap means of road transport before mass-produced vehicles became available.

1909 Daimler car chassis converted to a fire engine. This example was used by the Aldershot Volunteer Fire Brigade.

Daimler Show stand, circa 1912.

Company, who was suitably impressed with the terms and made his recommendation to accept at the Extraordinary General Meeting of the Daimler shareholders on October 10th 1910. The terms of the amalgamation, being a payment of £600,000 in cash and a share for share exchange, were approved with virtually no opposition. *The Daimler Company Limited* was formed with a new Board consisting of four BSA directors and three former Daimler directors.

Daimlers future stability seemed assured, but part of the arrangement with BSA had been that Daimler pay £100,000 per annum to BSA regardless of the cash available to do so. This resulted in an extended overdraft of £200,000 by February 1912. By 1914, this arrangement was causing serious problems once again.

The coming of the First World War had profound effects on both the Daimler and Lanchester companies.

In Lanchester's case, war effectively stopped the

manufacture of motor vehicles for some time. The War Office ordered the Lanchester Company to produce three-inch shrapnel shells, previously found to be effective during the Boer War. It took some time for the Military mind to discover that these were all but useless in trench warfare, so the War Office then ordered the production of 4.5 inch high-explosive shells! It took much persuading by Frank Lanchester that the Company's plant was unsuited to the production of shell cases, lacking heavy duty machine tools. In 1915, the powers that be finally relented and placed orders for 42 Armoured Cars, one which the Armourer Mills was far better suited to fulfill. This was followed by additional orders for high speed searchlight tenders, field kitchens and lumber wagons carrying winches for observation balloons, all based on the 38HP vehicle chassis. The most significant contribution to the war effort was the design and production of an advanced Armoured Car.

Lanchester Armoured Cars were built from 1915-1917 using 38HP chassis, engine and transmission,

Lanchester 38HP lorries.

but with reinforced suspension. Capable of 50mph, they compared very favourably with the more common Peerless vehicles, which had a maximum speed of 16mph. Thirty-six of the Lanchesters saw service on the Russian front, the remaining six being sunk en-route to Saudi Arabia, where they were to have supplemented Rolls-Royce vehicles.

Further contracts followed, paravanes (primitive mine sweepers), Constantinesco Interrupters (which syncronised machine guns with fighter propellers) and aero-engines.

George Lanchester later recalled that:

> "On conclusion of the war we had to re-establish our private trade and in 1918, when the Armistice was signed, we were caught without a line on paper towards a new design and our pre-war designs were obsolescent!"

The directors decided that the pre-war bonnetless designs had to go, there being little point in attempting to "educate the public to appreciate a car that is designed and produced strictly by adherence to the first logical principles of design". However, there were fewer buyers for the more expensive cars like Lanchesters. The old problem of under-capitalisation would soon begin, and at this juncture, the prospects were not good.

At the declaration of war on 4th August 1914, the Daimler Company was caught completely unawares, the entire workforce having departed on their annual holiday on July 31st.

Officials from the War Office commandeered every vehicle from the works within days. Demonstration cars, second-hand vehicles and unfinished vehicles were hastily assembled and driven to a mustering point in Hyde Park. A few days later orders for 20HP vehicles with box bodies were received. Sixty were manufactured and delivered between 7th and 18th August. An order for wagonettes followed, 50 being delivered by the end of October. In addition, 150 staff cars were delivered within three months and further orders for 600 limousines and 1,000 ambulances were placed by the War Office and private individuals, many of whom subsequently presented the ambulances to the War Office.

By 1916, the demand for cars fell and efforts were concentrated on the production of other vehicles. Commercial vehicles were adapted for war use, lorries of two, three, four and five tons capacity awaiting delivery to customers were commandeered and despatched to the front. Motor buses were removed from service in London at the rate of ten per week, refitted at Coventry and then sent abroad. A number of three-ton lorries were adapted as travelling workshops containing a six-inch lathe, a wet-tool grinder, a drill, vices, a forge and a set of hand tools. The total output of commercial vehicles in this period was over 4,000.

As a result of heavy demand for heavy duty tractors to pull 15-inch howitzers to emplacements at the front, a germ of an idea was developed into the design for the first tank. During trials at Lincoln it had been found that a bridging arrangement was required to allow the 105HP tractors to cross gulleys and ditches. A portable bridge was developed by William Foster & Co., but this was soon succeeded by a continuous travelling platform, or caterpillar track. Powered by a Daimler 105HP six-cylinder sleeve-valve engine and carrying 35 tons of armour, the tank first saw service on 15th September 1915 at the Battle of the Somme.

Other contributions to the war effort included shells and aero-engines, the first being the French-designed 80HP Rotary Gnome. With no clear idea about how to go about manufacturing these engines, an example was obtained, stripped, components measured and drawn, specifications compiled and production commenced within eight weeks!

By the end of 1918, the Company found itself with its plant worn out and scattered amongst temporary workshops, former employees laid-off and its commercial developments in a state of chaos. To attempt to stimulate the ailing motor car industry, the Society of Motor Manufacturers and Traders announced that it would hold its 13th Motor Show at Olympia during November 1919. The race was on to produce a new range of vehicles in time for the show!

The Daimler rotary Gnome aero-engine.

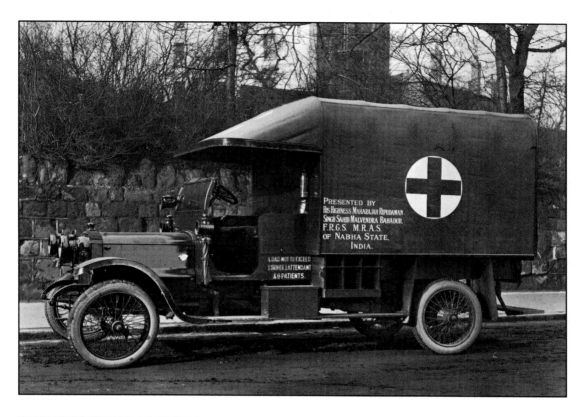

WARTIME DAIMLERS

The top photograph is easily recognised as an ambulance. The majority of Daimler Ambulances were constructed on the Daimler 20HP chassis. Although many vehicles were commandeered by the War Office, a significant number were donated by wealthy individuals or companies. The other vehicle is a mobile workshop, with lathes and workbence under the tarpaulin.

7. RECONSTRUCTION AND AMALGAMATION

"The great tragedy of the financial collapse of 1931 is that it need never have happened. There was no sudden disappearance of raw materials, credit, labour, skill and business sense, but financiers everywhere lost their heads"

Anthony Bird / Francis Hutton-Stott
Lanchester Motor Cars, 1964.

Work on a new 40HP Lanchester began early in 1919. A prototype was tested in August and production commenced shortly afterward. The new "Forty" was an overhead camshaft unit clearly influenced by aircraft designs. An advanced design by 1919 standards, it remained in production until 1929. The 1919 Show model was an unusual saloon, adorned with marquetry panelling to doors and roof, and was the most expensive car at the Motor Show. The fittings were so extravagant that George V was moved to remark: *"very fine Mr Lanchester, but more suited to a prostitute than a Prince, don't you think?"*.

The Forty was a direct rival of the Rolls-Royce Silver Ghost and was actively marketed as such. Press reports were encouraging and among the customers were Sir John Killerman (said to have been the richest man in England), the Duke of York (later George VI), and the Maharajah of Alwar. In 1921, prices were reduced from £2,200 to £1,800 to be £50 cheaper than the Ghost. In 1925 the Forty was first fitted with four-wheel brakes, a direct

response to rumours in 1924 that the next season's Ghost would be fitted with the same.

In 1921 Lanchester racing cars made their first appearance at Brooklands. T Hann's "Softly-Catch-Monkey", a modified 1911 38HP car won its third race and continued to race for a further four years. Lord Ridley's 1913 38HP achieved 90 mph beating the more modern racers such as Bentleys and Vauxhalls. A Lanchester Forty appeared in 1922, a standard chassis fitted with a two-seater racing body.

Another Forty was prepared by George Lanchester and A W Bird for Lionel Rapson to test his company's tyres to destruction. Driven by J G Parry-Thomas, the car broke 30 records in 15 hours and achieved an average of 104 mph for the last 100 miles.

In 1922, George Lanchester designed a new Armoured Car. Based on the 40HP engine and gearbox, the chassis was of armour plated girders allowing protection of the mechanical parts. A six-wheeled vehicle with four-wheel drive, the car had

"Winni-prap-praps", one of the legendary racing Lanchesters.

The Lanchester Armoured Car, as developed by George Lanchester in 1922. The car had six forward and reverse gears and a reinforced suspension for traversing rough terrain. After extensive testing by the military, these armoured cars saw service in many theatres of war. Unfortunately, after only twelve of the armoured cars had been delivered, the War Office cancelled their order, having revised their original plans to mechanize the 11th Hussars. By the time governmental interest revived, the Lanchester Company had been absorbed into Daimler.

exceptionally flexible suspension which allowed it to traverse rough terrain. Designed specifically as a fighting vehicle, the Armoured Car was accepted by the Mechanised Warfare Department, equipping the 11th Hussars and the 12th Lancers with twelve cars in 1931 after trials in 1922 and 1930. The 12th Lancers used the cars in Saar in 1934 and they later saw service in the early part of the Second World War.

1923 saw the development of the 21HP six-cylinder Lanchester, described as a "pup" off the Forty. Designed for the owner-driver, this car directly rivalled Rolls-Royce's 20HP "Gutless Wonder".

Sales of both the Forty and the 21HP did well during 1923-26, though the Forty lost ground to Rolls-Royce, who had meantime introduced a new model. Demand for "Gentlemen's Carriages" had begun to decline and Lanchester's were particularly vulnerable to a fluctuating market, being a low volume manufacturer with models in the luxury car class.

During the 1920s a growing middle class was providing a market for small cheap cars. These were provided by the likes of Henry Ford, William Morris and Herbert Austin. Well aware that this new market was there George and Frank Lanchester submitted designs for a small light car to the Board for four years. George Lanchester recalled that:

> "This design was revised from year to year in the light of development of current practice and re-submitted, but the Directors could not see the need for it - or would not provide the necessary financial support to launch such a venture."

A further Lanchester was developed in the 1920s, a luxury car, the 1928 30HP Straight-Eight, which received favourable press reports and was subsequently sold to an enviable list of distinguished customers. However, over-reliance on the carriage trade was to contribute to the Company's downfall and by 1929 the Lanchester Engine Company was again in financial difficulties.

Archie Millership, pictured at the wheel of a Lanchester 21HP.

Lanchester 40HP Tourer.

Lanchester 40HP seven-seater Landaulette.

Lanchester 21HP Drophead Coupe.

Daimler and BSA:
Shown here are an example of chassis and body styles from 1923. By this time the range of Daimler cars had become extremely complex and the cars featured here are with bodies by the factory. The 1920s BSAs were the Group's "entry model", but they were not very popular and failed to compete with the cheaper and more widely available mass-produced cars.

106-121-AOI

Type T.S., 30 h.p. Daimler Open Car
(5 or 7 seats.)

Construction.—Framing built of naturally seasoned ash mounted on Daimler patented body frame. Body panelled with hand beaten tinned steel. Two doors to front seat, two doors to rear seat. Safety catches to all doors to prevent them flying open if improperly latched.

Mounting.—Body is built on Daimler patented body frame and insulated from chassis by large rubber buffers, thereby protecting the body from road strain, and adding greatly to the comfort of the passengers.

Accommodation.—Two persons are accommodated on the front seat, and three on the rear seat. Where a seven seater car is required, two folding seats with back rests are provided.

Upholstery.—Upholstered to choice from wide range of highest quality leather. Cushions and seat profiles fitted with a spring case, and stuffed with selected horsehair. Rubber mats to front and rear footboards.

Weather Protection.—A balanced one-man type hood is fitted which, when erected, clamps to the top of the windscreen. The plate glass windscreen is divided, the lower part being fixed, the upper part adjustable. Convenient side curtains and a hood cover are also provided.

Finish.—Painted to choice from Daimler range of highest quality colours. Mouldings lined or plain as required. Wings, valances, petrol tank and road wheels black enamelled. Metal fittings nickel plated.

Price - £1,250   £1,265
(5 seats.)   (7 seats.)

A TABLE OF FITTINGS AND DIMENSIONS IS GIVEN OVERLEAF.

The Daimler Company Limited, Coventry.

Type F., 14 h.p. B.S.A. Two-Seater

Body.—The body provides two seats in front with ample leg room and width, and an extra passenger can be carried in the back when required. The car has been designed to combine utility and appearance and is essentially an any weather model. The side screens open with the door, and the rear side curtains fold into the hood when the hood is down. The seats and back are upholstered in blue, the tools being carried in a large locker under the seats. The body itself is coachbuilt with aluminium panels, and the painting and varnishing is carried out in accordance with coachwork practice. The standard colour is grey with polished aluminium bonnet, enamelled black wings, aluminium covered steps.

Windscreen.—Divided windscreen, lower part fixed, upper part adjustable.

The engine is a 4 cylinder water cooled sleeve-valve Daimler, built at the Daimler works, for a description of which see the chassis specification sheet.

Price - £285

A TABLE OF FITTINGS AND DIMENSIONS IS GIVEN OVERLEAF.

SOLE DISTRIBUTORS OF B.S.A. CARS - THE DAIMLER COMPANY LTD., COVENTRY

When the first post-war Motor Show opened on November 7th 1919, the Daimler Company was able to display two new models based on their six-cylinder 30HP and 45HP cars. These were offered on two wheelbases and designated "Light" Thirty and "Standard" Thirty. In the meantime, Daimler's management introduced a re-structuring of the Company's distribution network, which resulted in the new Daimlers being supplied by approved dealers rather than direct from the factory. This increased the efficiency of repair depots which now operated locally in close liaison with dealers. A hire service was provided with the formation of *Daimler Hire Limited*, which provided both self-drive and chauffeur-driven vehicles. This service was expanded with the provision of an air service between London and Paris in 1922 (later to become Imperial Airways). In 1927, a continental coach tour company was formed providing tours in sixteen-seater luxury Daimler Coaches fitted with coffee bars and on-board toilet facilities.

Reliability, comfort and finish were increasingly important issues for the motor manufacturers, particularly Daimler, which was now the pre-eminent luxury car manufacturer in Europe. Percy Martin, writing on 10th December 1924 noted that:

> *"we find every day that there is much greater interest being taken in the springing and perfect riding of the car than almost any other feature".*

Technological advances included the develop-ment of a lighter monobloc six-cylinder engine with detachable heads and steel rather than cast-iron sleeves. Increased strength in both engine and chassis allowed improved performance, so that four wheel brakes had to be introduced to provide more stopping power! The last four-cylinder Daimler car was produced in 1921, thereafter succeeded by a 3 litre six-cylinder the following year. Six-cylinder cars gained in popularity. In 1925, 27% of the exhibits at the Motor Show were powered by six-cylinder units, by 1928, this proportion had increased to 44%.

However, rivals such as Rolls-Royce had introduced new models whose engine technology was considerably in advance of the ageing Knight sleeve-valve engines. A new Daimler was needed to maintain the lead in the luxury car market. Since smooth and silent power were very much the order of the day, the decision was taken to develop Britain's first V-12 engine.

The development of the new engine was entrusted to Lawrence Pomeroy, one of the most distinguished and respected of Britain's designers. Pomeroy had worked previously at Vauxhall where he had been chief designer since 1912. Following the end of the First World War, he had decided to leave Vauxhall. Hearing of this, Frederick Lanchester had written to Percy Martin urging him to recruit Pomeroy at Daimler:

> *"If I had shares in Vauxhall I would sell them quick. It was as near a one-man show as anything in the country!"*

The Daimler 6-45HP Special, with body by Maythorn for an Indian Maharajah.

Daimler Hire:
"Hire - By Land, Sea and Air". Daimler Hire developed from a limousine hire service started on November 10th, 1907, and was registered as a seperate limited company in 1920. In 1923, the Company was granted a Royal Warrant as Motor Car Hirers to King George V and retained the Royal Warrant until the 1960s. In 1930, the cash-starved BSA Group sold part of its interest in Daimler Hire to the Thomas Tillings Group, who commenced a self-drive hire service in 1931. The fleet peaked at 400 chauffeur-driven limousines and 100 self-drive cars in the mid-1930s. Thomas Tillings acquired the whole of the Company in 1947, and it was later sold to Hertz in 1958.

It was not until 1925 that Pomeroy joined Daimler, where he was appointed Chief Engineer and later promoted to Managing Director in 1929. Under Pomeroy's management the new V-12 was derived from an existing six-cylinder 25/85HP Daimler engine. Four blocks of three were formed on a common crankcase to make a 60 degree V-12 unit of 7,136cc. The new "Double-Six" was offered with three different lengths of wheelbase, with high and low radiators, allowing the widest possible scope for coachbuilders. At the 1926 Motor Show a Double-Six 50 was shown, with coachwork finished in two shades of grey.

In 1928, a smaller version of the car was introduced, the Double-Six 30. Despite the size and high price of the vehicle, the Double-Six was a modest success during the recession of the late 1920s. Amongst the Company's customers was His Majesty the King, who had Double-Six units fitted to the existing Royal Daimlers (dating from 1913) as well as ordering several new cars for the Royal Mews.

However competition continued to be severe between Daimler, Rolls-Royce, Bentley and other luxury car manufacturers. Towards the end of the 1920s all these firms suffered from increasing financial hardship. Daimler in particular was badly hit, with sales falling in 1927 and 1928, taking the company into deficit. 1929 saw no improvement in financial performance and the company paid no dividends to shareholders until after 1936. The return to profitability in 1936 was welcomed but the company's largest profits of the decade amounted to just over £10,000 in 1937.

Although this was partly due to a downturn in what was an increasingly limited market, production and distribution methods in the 1920s had fallen behind those adopted by their competitors. Part of this malaise was a result of retaining the sleeve-valve engine beyond its useful life, part was due to the extravagant range of twenty-three different models (exclusive of the bodies available), five engine types and twelve chassis types which placed upward pressure on unit costs and a poor pricing policy and lack of capital expenditure on items such as machine tools, where only £70,000 was spent during the entire 1920s.

A report commissioned by BSA in 1929 on its subsidiary companies was highly critical of the use of *Stratton-Instone* as the sole distributors for Daimler cars. Although this had been an improvement on the previous practice of supplying direct from the factory, the commission rate of 20 - 25 per cent was unduly high and had a depressing effect on sales. This view was confirmed by the company's bankers in 1931 who concluded that "there is no doubt price has something to do with this as well as performance." The arrangement had resulted from Ernest Instone's links with Daimler first as Company Secretary and later as General Manager, but by 1932 BSA had exerted sufficient pressure on the Daimler Board to terminate this privileged arrangement and seek a wider range of distributors.

The board itself was subject to considerable criticism, having failed to rectify the increasingly obvious problems which had beset the company since the end of the First World War. Writing to Percy Martin in 1931, former BSA director E M Griffith was quite clear about the primary reason for this state of affairs:

> "The old style Board of Directors is out of date; it has had its trial since the war and has been found wanting. The unfortunate system of appointing directors having no knowledge of the business has been tolerated too long in this country, and a director serving on multiple companies is a great source of weakness."

In 1929, Pomeroy was appointed Managing Director of the Company, Percy Martin becoming Chairman. On Martin's initiative, a new form of transmission was developed and was to be a contributing factor to the Company's recovery in the 1930s. Fluid-flywheel transmission enabled the driver to engage and disengage the transmission without the use of a clutch. The transmission also allowed the car to travel at very slow speeds, a difficult thing to achieve with a crash gearbox.

To demonstrate and publicise the system a series of films was commissioned, *Bringing up Grandma*, *Pa Puts His Foot Down* and *Roadwards*. Using actors and animation, the films featured Daimlers, Lanchesters and BSAs fitted with the transmission. In *Roadwards* there is a particularly memorable scene where a test driver engages first gear, sets the car running, then gets out of the car, walks round, gets in and continues driving. Though a staged demonstration, this did show the advantages of the system, particularly to the funeral and carriage trades.

Demonstrating the transmission at Motor Shows was another matter. John Speed, a Daimler employee at the time, recalled in *The Driving Member* how the Company went about this:

> "Someone, I know not who, conceived the bright idea of constructing a driving and driven member with a wire mesh casing. Inside was placed a number of tennis balls. When the driven member was rotated by an electric motor, the tennis balls would take up the path of the oil and all would be made clear? The contraption was approximately 3 feet in diameter and it worked for three or four revolutions; after which the tennis balls would get in a boggle-boggle in one or two of the spiral compartments and occasionally one would break away for as little trip round on its own. When they all got nicely stuck one ball would occasionally squeeze between the driving and driven member and shoot off as if from a pop gun, into the great open spaces of Olympia and hit someone important like Mr Dunlop"

The financial crisis of 1930-31 had its origins in the loss of market confidence which followed the Wall Street Crash of October 1929. This had profound repercussions on both the Daimler and Lanchester companies.

Lawrence Pomeroy, designer of Vauxhall racing cars, pictured in 1914 at the wheel of a Vauxhall Grand Prix Racing Car.

Visit to the Daimler works by the directors in 1930. From left to right, Bertie Herbert, Percy Martin, 4th from left Patric Hannon, extreme right F W Hancock.

1 This picture shows a metal bowl filled with oil and provided with vanes. The bowl is fitted with a vertical spindle which can be driven round by the pulley and belt shown.

2 Here we see the bowl being spun round. It is obvious that as the speed of rotation increases the oil will be flung upwards and outwards from the bowl which will rapidly empty itself.

3 Suppose we fill the b place immediately ov kind. When the lov be flung up and round causing this to rotate in th

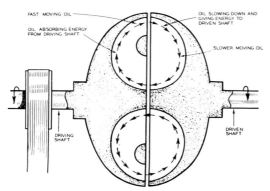

FAST MOVING OIL

OIL SLOWING DOWN AND GIVING ENERGY TO DRIVEN SHAFT

OIL ABSORBING ENERGY FROM DRIVING SHAFT

SLOWER MOVING OIL

DRIVING SHAFT

DRIVEN SHAFT

6 Here we see the two bowls illustrated in Fig. 5 turned into a horizontal position. It can be seen now how energy is transferred from one bowl to the other. The oil takes up energy from the driving bowl as it flows from the centre to the rim and delivers up energy to the driven bowl as it passes from the circumference to the centre.

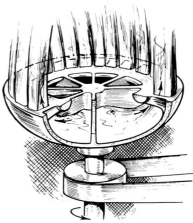

7 By shaping the pockets in the driving bowl like this and driving the shaft at a high speed the oil is thrown out in jets.

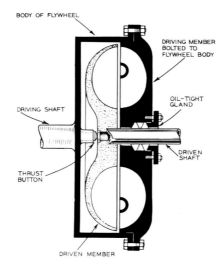

BODY OF FLYWHEEL

DRIVING MEMBER BOLTED TO FLYWHEEL BODY

OIL-TIGHT GLAND

DRIVING SHAFT

DRIVEN SHAFT

THRUST BUTTON

DRIVEN MEMBER

8 In the arrangement shown in illustration 6 above, very considerable end thrust would be set up on the driving and driven shafts. By interchanging the driving member and driven member as here shown it is possible to insert a thrust button which allows these two end thrusts to neutralise each other.

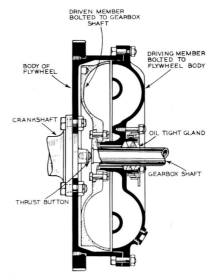

DRIVEN MEMBER BOLTED TO GEARBOX SHAFT

DRIVING MEMBER BOLTED TO FLYWHEEL BODY

BODY OF FLYWHEEL

CRANKSHAFT

OIL TIGHT GLAND

THRUST BUTTON

GEARBOX SHAFT

9 Here is an actual section of the Daimler Fluid Flywheel as used on the B.S.A. 10-h.p. Car. After you have examined the previous illustrations it requires no explanation. Notice the shapes of the driving and driven members and the thrust button.

10

10B

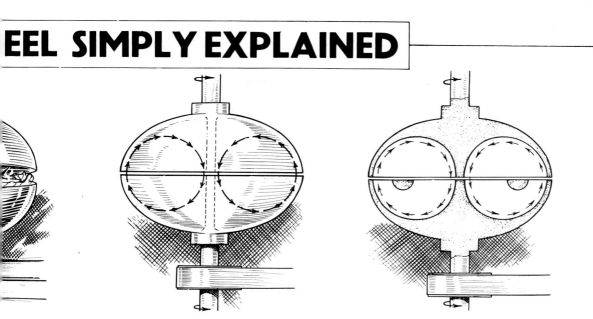

4 The oil inside the two bowls will by now be circulating from the upper to the lower bowl as shown by the arrows.

5 As the object of the lower bowl is to project jets of oil into the upper bowl, the interior pockets in the two bowls should obviously be shaped something like this to conform with the path of oil.

he driven member with used in the Daimler Fluid to the B.S.A. 10,h.p. Car.

photograph of the driving the Daimler Fluid Fly-with illustration 7 above.

fore spinning we
bowl of the same
round the oil will
bowl gradually
s the lower bowl.

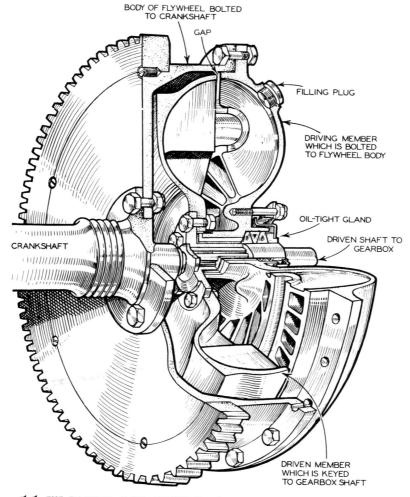

BODY OF FLYWHEEL BOLTED TO CRANKSHAFT

GAP

FILLING PLUG

DRIVING MEMBER WHICH IS BOLTED TO FLYWHEEL BODY

OIL-TIGHT GLAND

DRIVEN SHAFT TO GEARBOX

CRANKSHAFT

DRIVEN MEMBER WHICH IS KEYED TO GEARBOX SHAFT

11 THE DAIMLER FLUID FLYWHEEL AS USED ON THE B.S.A. 10-H.P. CAR.
This shows a pictorial section of the flywheel. Note that the driving member is provided with specially shaped pockets as illustrated in Fig. 10ᴮ. The driven member is provided with radial vanes which catch the jets of oil thrown from the rim of the driving member and return it to the centre.

The BSA Group had already undertaken an enforced economy drive, which included the termination of Frederick Lanchester's consultancy in 1929 and the closing of *Lanchester Laboratories Limited*, a company set up with the object of developing his inventions and carrying out research and development work.

This dismissal resulted in some acrimony between Lanchester and the Company, which accused him of spending too much of his time and the Company's money researching irrelevances.

Further dismissals were forthcoming in the bodyshop, which was also closed in 1929, although this proved to be a false economy, with £40,000 worth of unusable coachwork having to be scrapped. As well as cost savings, steps were taken to realise liquid assets. Daimler's share in Singer was gradually run down and in 1931, Daimler Hire was sold off to help reduce the Company's overdraft. Car production virtually ceased, and, for a short time in 1931, commercial vehicle and aero-engine manufacture were the Company's only activities.

However, the Lanchester Company got into even more serious trouble. Constrained by a range of cars which catered for the carriage trade and only the richest of owner-drivers, the Company was one of the first to be hit by the belt-tightening that followed the 1929 crash.

Had the Company developed a smaller, cheaper car it is entirely possible that it could have ridden out the crisis as Daimler did, but chronic under-capitalisation had resulted in dependence on an overdraft for day-to-day financing. This hard core of short-term finance fluctuated between £40,000 and £50,000, the equivilant of 30 cars on the road. The Company's bankers, losing their nerve, called in the overdraft at short notice. In a market where financiers and investors had lost heavily, the Company was unable to raise the necessary finance and faced closure in a matter of weeks.

The BSA Group put in an offer to acquire the business. Bird and Hutton-Stott in *Lanchester Motor Cars* gave the following account of the proceedings:

"With bewildering speed therefore, the transaction was put in hand; like rabbits hypnotised by bright lights, the Lanchester Board agreed to terms which left it entirely to Daimlers to decide what kind of motor car should bear the name of Lanchester...Frank Lanchester became a Sales Director (without authority) with the new Lanchester division of the Daimler Company, and George Lanchester became a member of their senior design staff. With the exception of the Service Manager, Mr Aston, all the rest of the Lanchester team, many of whom had

Daimler widely advertised the fluid-flywheel transmission, which provided almost effortless gearchanges compared to the contemporary crash 'boxes.

been with the company since it started, became redundant...only there was no such thing as severance pay or redundancy compensation in 1931"

Stock and plant were removed from the Birmingham factory to Daimler at Coventry, many of the spares for the earlier cars being scrapped. Leaving aside Bird and Hutton-Stott's somewhat partisan view, there was hardly place for separate production facilities and the Lanchester design and production function was from then on controlled by Daimler.

Daimler paid £26,000 for Lanchester, a small price for a prestige car manufacturer, even in 1931. By any standards the speed of the takeover was quite remarkable and there has been suspicion that Lanchester's bankers colluded with the BSA Board. Writing in *Dudley Docker*, R T P Davenport-Hines speculated that *"there must be a suspicion that the extensive influence of the BSA directors was behind the bank's decision to recall the loan and trigger the Lanchester cash crisis..."*

The take-over of Lanchester was fortuitously timed, since Daimler desperately needed access to the smaller car market but was conscious that use of the Daimler name alone would compromise the firm's reputation with its customers for its luxury vehicles. Takeover provided the opportunity to remove a competitor from the latter market and utilise that competitor's reputation for build quality and innovation to break into a volume market. It almost certainly prevented the premature demise of both marques and, according to Percy Martin, rescued the Daimler company from total collapse during the exceptionally grim period of 1931-32.

The last of the Lanchester Straight-Eights was sold as new in 1933. George Lanchester remained with the Group until 1936, when he moved to Alvis to take up a position as fighting vehicle development engineer.

Frederick Lanchester suffered badly from the closure of Lanchester Laboratories, but continued with his experimental activities, seriously hampered in the mid-1930s by the onset of Parkinson's disease and cataracts in both eyes. His lack of commercial acumen had a direct consequence towards the end of his life when he was unable to afford one of his own cars . However, he continued to publish papers on a variety of subjects until 1942. Awarded the James Watt medal in 1945 by the Institution of Mechanical Engineers, he was too ill to collect the award personally and died on 8th March 1946 at the age of 77. *The Autocar*, on reviewing thirty-six modern characteristics of the modern car, attributed at least eighteen of them directly to Lanchester's theories and designs.

George Lanchester continued with Alvis through the Second World War and was retained by the Sterling Armament Company as a consulting engineer. In 1961, he retired at the age of 87. His retirement was spent writing articles, taking an active part in motoring organisations and even a little inventing. An active patron of the Daimler & Lanchester Owners Club and the Lanchester Register, his death at the age of 95 on 13th February 1970 was sudden and unexpected.

A still from the film "Roadwards", showing the Daimler Fifteen assembly line.

Fluid-flywheel transmission was fitted to the post-acquisition Lanchester range of cars, and this Lanchester 15/18 limousine was bodied by Abbotts of Farnham.

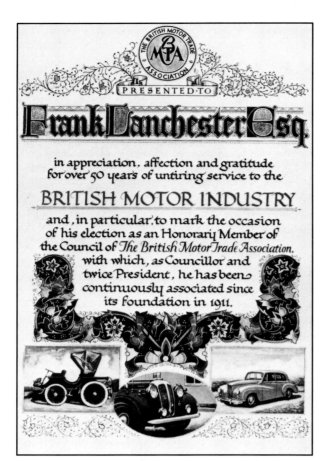

Percy Martin, General Manager
and later Chairman of Daimler.

Frank Lanchester.   George Lanchester.

Frank Lanchester's work in the British motor industry was
widely recognised in the trade, but not elsewhere.

Frank Lanchester, though overshadowed by the engineering parts of the Unholy Trinity, was the business man who built up the early Lanchester Company on good faith and attention to detail (he never let a letter go unanswered) which enabled him to sell the cars against stiff opposition whilst with Lanchester and subsequently as the Sales Director of the Lanchester division of Daimler. He died on March 28th 1960.

The last purely "Lanchester" design was the 15/18 which set the style for the Daimlers of the 1930s. Powered by a 2.5 litre six-cylinder engine with overhead poppet-valves, the design suited the owner-driver admirably, featuring the Wilson preselect gearbox with fluid-flywheel transmission, which would be fitted to most Daimlers and Lanchesters until the late 1950s.

Although George Lanchester worked with Lawrence Pomeroy during the early thirties, Lanchester cars were soon to be wholly designed by Daimler. Though of undoubtedly sound design, economies of scale meant that they did not really bear comparison with the earlier "strict" Lanchesters in terms of performance or refinement. Bird and Hutton-Stott were less than complimentary:

"Refined but dull was the common verdict and "old ladies car" a familiar gibe. Consequently the Lanchester cars of the time were too often seen piloted in a rather haphazard way at 25mph on the crown of the road, while their elderly conductors chatted brightly to the passengers, sublimely unconscious of the traffic behind or ahead-"

In the final analysis, the -use of the Lanchester name in this way was to lead to its eventual demise. Customers for the Lanchesters of the 1920s must have been disappointed and these smaller cars never sold as well as anticipated.

The Lanchester Motor Company still exists. It has its registered office at Jaguar Cars Limited, Browns Lane, Coventry. Although a dormant company, the name came close to being revived in 1982 when Jaguar Cars entered into discussions with Ford on the subject of importing and distributing Jaguars into Germany. It was proposed that a badge-engineered Jaguar would be marketed as a Lanchester , since the use of the Daimler name in Germany was precluded by the presence of its distant cousin, Daimler-Benz. Market research, conducted by Joe Greenwell at Jaguar Cars, soon revealed confusion with the Lancaster bomber and Burt Lancaster and the idea was dropped.

8. THE AGE OF THE OWNER-DRIVER

"Verily, these were splendid motor-carriages, but they did belong to an age of grandeur and affluence which is unlikely to return."

William Boddy
The Daimler Double-Sixes
1966

In the early 1900s, purchase of a motor vehicle involved further, additional, expense. One had to employ a chauffeur, who doubled as a mechanic. A fully equipped workshop was required and, in the days when petrol could only be purchased from the chemist by the pint, construction of a fireproof storage system was essential. Further, if your chauffeur was not familiar with your chosen vehicle, he had to be despatched to the factory to learn how to drive it.

Gradually the ability of the general public to operate motor vehicles became more widespread, firstly as the result of the gradual introduction of public service and commercial vehicles, particularly from 1909 when Knight's design for the sleeve-valve engine was adopted and widely accepted by the municipal authorities.

If nothing else, the First World War was responsible for many thousands of men and women learning how to operate and maintain motor vehicles. This was a direct result of the enormous output throughout the war of all forms of mechanised transport from manufacturers and the final displacement of the horse as the main means of motive power in the first weeks of the conflict. By the end of the war the public perception of motor cars had changed and vast numbers of ex-servicemen returned and bought motor vehicles after being de-mobilised.

Much of this demand was catered for by the volume manufacturers, particularly Henry Ford, William Morris and Herbert Austin, who all produced, for the first time, cars which were within the reach of the ordinary working man. Motor manufacturers who had originally supplied the carriage trade, the nobility and the monied classes gradually became aware of a growing professional and middle class who, whilst unable to afford and buy and run large and expensively appointed vehicles, demanded much more refinement than

The Daimler Double-Six with Lawrence Pomeroy's newly-designed V12 poppet-valve engine, which replaced the ageing sleeve-valve based on Knight's designs. This magnificent example was bodied by Charlesworth, the coachbuilders.

provided by the "Tin-Lizzie" and its rivals. The new market came to the fore in the 1920s and 1930s, when demand was for small high-class cars which could be run economically .

The Daimler Company was, unlike Lanchester, fortunate in being able to respond to this demand. Replacing the ageing sleeve-valve designs with the now advanced poppet-valve design developed by Lanchester, in October 1932 an entirely new model, the Daimler Fifteen, was announced. Powered by an all-new 1805cc six-cylinder overhead valve engine with the new fluid-flywheel transmission, the car was able to move away without the snatch and jerk so commonplace then and provided smooth and silent gearchanges, anticipating the automatic transmission systems which were to succeed it over twenty years later.

From 1932 to 1936 the sleeve-valve engines were gradually phased out and the Fifteen was revised and improved. In 1934, the introduction of an enlarged 2003cc engine and improved chassis and steering, together resulted in a top speed of around 70mph and fuel consumption of 24-25 miles per gallon. The Fifteen was again revised in 1937, the engine enlarged to 2166cc and yet again in 1938 to 2522cc.

Daimler's Lanchester models were confined to the small to medium size and price range, the first being the 15/18HP of 1931. The Lanchester "Ten", the cheapest available car in the range fitted with fluid-flywheel transmission, was introduced in 1932 and

evolved into the Lanchester "Eleven" in 1936. The range was supplemented in 1937 by the introduction of the 1527cc Lanchester "Roadrider", a name that emphasised the car's advanced suspension and excellent roadholding qualities.

The carriage trade was not neglected and the sleeve-valved "Double-Six" was replaced with something new. The acquisition of the Lanchester Company had been fortuitous in this respect since they had independently developed an advanced straight-eight power unit of 4440cc capable of powering a large luxury car to speeds in excess of 89mph. The late David Scott-Moncrieff, "Purveyor of Horseless Carriages to the Nobility and Gentry", later described this as the sweetest engine encountered in his career.

Lawrence Pomeroy appropriated the best features of this engine to the design of the new Daimler engine, though a more advanced valve and carburettor arrangement was developed. The result was an engine which was characterised by noiselessness and absence of vibration, with little indication that the vehicle was mechanically propelled.

It was well suited to the carriage trade, though later supplied to the more discerning and wealthy owner-driver. The combination of the straight-eight engine and the fluid-flywheel transmission soon found favour with several Royal Houses, both at home and abroad. Designated V26 by the factory, the Straight-Eight models served at State occasions

The Lanchester Eleven was a development of the Lanchester Ten. These small but refined saloons were aimed to provide the BSA Group with a market for smaller mass-produced cars.

An early example of "badge-engineering". This 1938 Lanchester was a restyled Daimler, provided at the request of George VI.

for over twenty years. A number of these Daimlers were produced as Lanchesters for the Duke of York, (later King George VI), and the Maharajah of Nawanagar.

Towards the end of the 1930s advances in chassis design, valve technology and engine performance resulted in the development of the Daimler "Dolphin". In 1938, after a break of over thirty years from competition and racing, Daimlers began to feature in the Monte Carlo Rally and in the English, Scottish and Welsh Rallies. Bob Crouch and George Fabel in the Dolphin were later joined by C M Simpson in an EL24 in the 1939 RAC Rally. However, these activities were to be cut short with the coming of the Second World War.

This time, the British Motor Industry was better prepared for war. With the rise of fascist dictatorships in Europe in the 1920s and 1930s, Stanley Baldwin's government had concentrated on the prospect of war and in particular on the need to adapt the country's industrial base to wartime production in the event of prolonged hostilities. By February 1936, the cabinet had resolved to enter into a programme of development for the Royal Air Force which would involve the manufacture of some 8,000 new fighter and bomber aircraft. Both government and industry perceived the need for additional facilities if these ambitious plans were ever to be realised.

A meeting was convened for May 1936, to be chaired by the Secretary of State for Air and its

The Daimler Fifteen was popular with coachbuilders. This 1935 Cabriolet was bodied by Salmons Tickford.

participants included Sir Geoffrey Burton of Daimler, John Black of Standard, Spencer Wilks of Rover and Lord Austin. The result of these discussions was the commencement of the Shadow Factory Schemes and it was agreed the Daimler, Standard, Rover, Austin and Bristol companies combine to mass-produce aircraft engines. In contrast to the previous war, the companies were left very much to their own devices without undue interference from the War Office. By 1937 the scheme had been put in place.

The new factories were Government financed and equipped, and the motor manufacturers were paid a fee for their services as managing agents. Aircraft production was entirely separate from existing motor manufacturing facilities although in practice Daimler's new facilities were located close to its main works in Capmartin Road.

With the coming of the Second World War, heavy bombing raids by the Luftwaffe were aimed at destroying Britain's industrial infrastructure and demoralising the population. Coventry suffered particularly badly from the Blitz, losing much of the city centre (including its ancient cathedral). During October and November 1940 both Daimler Shadow Factories were badly hit, with considerable damage to the buildings and grounds. However, they were able to continue production with little disruption. Incendiary bombing on the night of April 8th, 1941 resulted in virtual destruction of the main Radford works and Shadow Factory Number One, but despite this setback, production was back up to pre-raid levels by the summer, the Company's activities being relocated to 44 dispersal factories.

Although wartime production included gun turrets, aero-engines, gun parts, rocket projectors and wartime utility vehicles, Daimler's own particular contribution was the development of the Daimler Scout Car and the Daimler Armoured car.

Discussions first took place between the Army and the Company in spring 1938. Exacting requirements were given by the Military for the design and production of a high-speed vehicle

The Daimler Dolphin was developed as the Daimler Fifteen gradually became more powerful and refined.

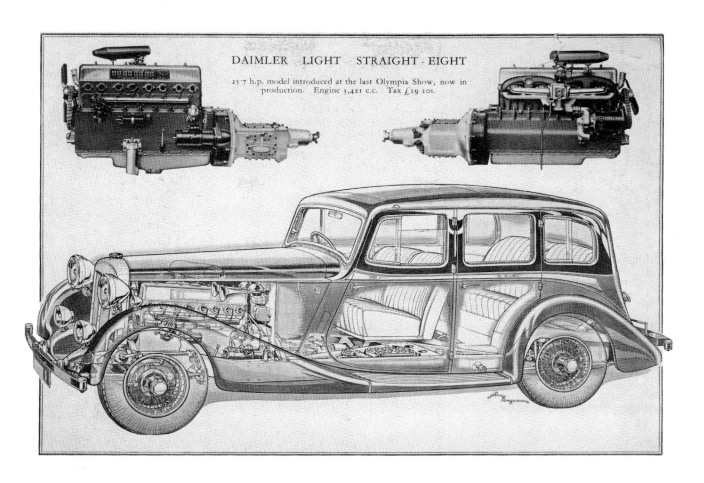

DAIMLER LIGHT STRAIGHT - EIGHT

25·7 h.p. model introduced at the last Olympia Show, now in production. Engine 3,421 c.c. Tax £19 10s.

The Daimler Light Straight-Eight. Aimed specifically at the richer owner-driver, this fine example was bodied by Vanden Plas.

Bob Crouch, pictured with a Daimler Dolphin. This car performed well on the Monte Carlo Rally, and featured in the English, Scottish and Welsh Rallies just prior to the Second World War, when Daimler's newly revived rallying programme was cut short.

capable of travelling over bomb craters, negotiating ditches, driving over high obstacles and fording rivers. The vehicle would have to be capable of climbing gradients of 1 in 2 as well as travelling at speed along ordinary roads.

In September 1938, barely six months after the first meeting, a prototype "Scout" car was handed to the Army. Using a six-cylinder engine of 2522cc, fluid-flywheel transmission and all-round independent suspension, the Scout Car proved to be precisely what was required and a firm order was placed with the factory in May 1939. The first batch was delivered in December 1939 and altogether 6,665 Scout Cars were produced and saw active service in all the theatres of the Second World War.

The Daimler Armoured Car was produced in smaller quantities, 2,734 in total. Powered by a 4095cc six-cylinder engine, the seven-ton Armoured Car was fitted with disc-brakes and four-wheel drive. Despite its weight, the vehicle was capable of speeds of over fifty miles per hour.

At the end of the war rumours abounded of Daimler ceasing production of private cars. This was officially denied in September 1945 when Daimler announced that production of the pre-war 2.5 litre Daimler Fifteen would commence, the car now being redesignated DB18. By 1946, production had also resumed of a considerably redesigned Daimler Straight-Eight, the DE27, and of the new Lanchester 10.

Victory Parade, Tunis, May 20th, 1943

Daimler
goes to war

AIMLER COMPANY LIMITED · LONDON AND COVENTRY

"Daimler Goes to War". A series of advertisements taken by the Company featuring the Daimler Scout Car and the Daimler Armoured Car.

WARTIME DAIMLERS

Of special importance to the war efforts in the Second World War were the Daimler Armoured Cars and the Daimler Scout Cars. The Scout Car was developed in 1938 and featured the Daimler DB18 engine as well as all-round independent suspension and Daimler fluid-flywheel transmission. The Armoured Cars were powered by a six cylinder 4095cc engine with twin Solex carburettors. Other features included wading equipment and disc brakes. Both vehicles saw service in all theatres of war and were held in the highest esteem by the Military.

9. THE DOCKERS

"All I ever wanted to do was to put the name Daimler on the lips of everyone. People hated me for that, but I was determined not to let the name die."

Lady Norah Docker,
1983.

The name of Docker had been associated with the Daimler Company for many years. F Dudley Docker, father of Bernard, was made a director in 1910, resigning in 1912 to join the BSA Board, where he served until his death in 1944.

Bernard Docker was born in 1896. On leaving Harrow he joined the *Metropolitan Carriage, Wagon and Finance Company Limited*, a subsidiary of the BSA Group. By 1920 he had been appointed Chairman of a sister company, *The Metropolitan Carriage Company*. Later knighted, Sir Bernard Docker joined the Daimler Board in 1940 and was elected Chairman of the BSA Group on 22 December 1941 at the age of 45. An active businessman, he was also chairman of a number of concerns with connections in the banking and insurance world.

The post-war BSA Group controlled several coachbuilders as well as the Daimler and Lanchester companies including *Hooper & Co.* (the Royal Coachbuilders), *Carbodies* and *Barkers*, which helped Daimler retain their position as pre-eminent manufacturers of large, well-appointed cars. The Daimler DE36, powered by an enormous 5460cc straight-eight engine was added to the range in 1946. It was then the largest British production chassis, with a wheelbase of 12 feet 3 inches, which resulted in a car over eighteen feet long. With this limousine and the smaller six-cylinder Daimler DE27, the Company enjoyed renewed success, supplying new cars to the Royal Mews, a fleet of cars for the Royal Tour of South Africa in 1947 and the Royal Tour of Australia and New Zealand in 1953. Middle-range cars consisted of the Daimler DB18, later succeeded by the Daimler Consort with the Lanchester LD10 as the "entry model" to the Company's range.

In February 1949, Bernard Docker married Norah Collins, a former dancer and a formidable lady who was by then marrying her third millionaire. A forceful character, she exerted considerable influence over both Sir Bernard and the policy of the Daimler Company. In her book, *Norah, the Autobiography of Lady Docker*, she later said:

"I was ashamed when I married Bernard, to discover that, both at home and abroad, the superb Daimler car was in danger of becoming a relic. As my husband was the head of the Daimler Company - a subsidiary of the Birmingham Small Arms Group, of which he was Chairman - I induced him to re-examine the Company's marketing policies. I told him 'the only people who know about Daimler are the Royal family! I know you could not find better customers, Bernard, but Daimler cannot survive on status alone. It's got to sell to the masses.'"

June 1950 saw the production of a special Hooper-bodied 2 1/2 litre for her ladyship. This was a modest car of elegant proportions, but something more extravagant was contemplated for the forthcoming London Motor Show.

Lady Docker, now appointed to the Hooper Board, aimed to produce vehicles which would attract favourable publicity for Daimler. From 1950 to 1955, she was responsible for the production of a series of spectacular and exotic Daimlers which appeared at succeeding Motor Shows.

There was considerable expense in this course as each vehicle was hand-built for the show and was never intended for mass-production. In this she was assisted by Osmond Rivers, Hooper's principal designer, who translated her extravagant ideas into exotic vehicles for each motor show. This was no easy task since Norah Docker was a demanding "client" who would summons Rivers to her Mayfair flat at short notice to deal with some minor aspect of design, often involving fabrics which were more suited to ball gowns than car interiors.

The first of the so-called "Docker" Daimlers was a Straight-Eight Sedanca de Ville, with Hooper coachwork painted ivory over black with the rear compartment trimmed in a special white cloth. It certainly attracted the attention and publicity intended, and the *London Sunday Express* commented:

"The most beautiful thing I have seen recently is a motor car. Created jointly by the Royal coachbuilders and the

Post-War Daimler DB18s:
Production of the Daimler DB18 recommenced in 1947. Apart from the DB18 saloon (also known as the Daimler 2½ litre), there were a number of variations based around the same basic chassis design. This Hooper-bodied Daimler Special Sports featured an electrically-operated hood and an exceptionally high level of interior appointments. The car was originally commissioned by King Farouk of Egypt.

This 1949 Fixed-Head Coupe was bodied by Daimler.

The Daimler DB18 saloon.

The Daimler Consort. A development of the DB18, the styling was a compromise between the pre- and post-war designs, retaining a shape reminiscent of the late 1930s but with integral headlamps.

The Daimler DE36 was the largest British post-war production car. *The Motor* described it *as a car of such striking performance and qualities that one searches almost in vain, for the appropriate adjective. Possibly "fabulous" is the most embracing term for a car that is considerably the most expensive in the world, has the largest wheelbase and the biggest body space of any European car, has all the qualities of silence and dignity of which Daimler is a synonym with speed acceleration and roadholding which would evoke praise in a sports model.* This example was produced with coachwork by Freestone & Webb for a wealthy Jamaican customer.

Another Daimler DE36, with coachwork by Hooper. This example was built for the Royal Household.

Daimler DE36 limousine by Hooper.

Royal car makers, it is a superb and unashamed example of non-austerity."

It concluded that:

"*Certainly Lady Docker's journeys should not be dull. She can enjoy a drink from an electrically operated cocktail cabinet; make up her face with the aid of a silver equipped vanity case; listen to a five station radio concealed in the arm-rest; take a book or magazine from a hidden shelf; and see - or be seen - by fluorescent illumination.*"

The next was the 1951 Gold car, designed by Osmond Rivers and based on the Daimler DE36 chassis. Lady Docker later recalled:

"*I had trouble with this car...we thought about brass. Cast brass would have been too expensive to use. Mr Rivers then said it would be cheaper to use steel and dip, not plate, everything in gold. So we did. The trouble was that every time we touched the gold parts, the metal wore off and had to be re-dipped for each showing.*"

The car caused a sensation at the 1951 Motor Show. In attracting publicity it undoubtedly achieved what it set out to do and for a time, Daimler became a household name. *The Motor* commented "the most magnificent car in the world". *The Daily Mirror*, reflecting a more populist view, featured the car with the headline " PLEASE DON'T CALL MY GOLD PLATED CAR VULGAR, PLEADS LADY DOCKER".

The Daily Mirror may have had a point. Finished in black and gold, the car was black above the waistline and black with tiny gold stars in the panels which had been painstakingly applied star by star by Geoffrey Francis, heraldic artist by Royal appointment. Every part of the car, inside and out, which would have otherwise been chromium-plated was finished in gold. The headlining and upholstery was finished in gold silk by Warners of London and the gold and crystal picnic fittings were by Cartier of Bond Street. Specially-made black crocodile-hide suitcases were mounted in gold in the boot and lined with gold silk. Even the controls for the concealed radio were gold-plated. There was no doubt that the vehicle was astonishingly ostentatious and the standard of craftsmanship involved was superlative.

A second DE36 car was requisitioned and work began on the 1952 exhibit. Not dissimilar to the

"The Green Goddess" was the 1948 Daimler Show car built on a DE36 chassis, with coachwork by Hooper.

Gold Car, this time the car was finished in powder blue and grey, and, perhaps in response to the jibes of the press the previous year, fittings were finished in a more restrained chrome. Inside, the car furnishings were in a blue-grey lizard skin, including the steering-wheel cover, and the interior fittings were broadly similar to those on the previous year's car. This car was designed for the owner-driver, albeit one who regularly was in attendance at the French Riviera, where the Dockers maintained an ocean-going luxury yacht.

The 1953 exhibit was built on the new 3 litre chassis. Lighter than the previous cars, bodywork was of aluminium. Lady Docker recalled:

> "I was never satisfied with this car (it had originally been finished in green). I asked Mr Rivers to change it to a metallic silver-blue. When the press asked me what it was called, I remembered the BSA Golden Flash motorbike and said 'Silver Flash'"

Upholstery was in more conventional black leather with red piping, but the instrument panel, suitcases and the remainder of the trim was finished in red crocodile skin.

The 1954 car, constructed on the new Daimler DK400 chassis, was given similar treatment to the 1951 Gold Car, but finished in Royal Blue with chrome rather than gold being used throughout.

The Docker Daimler "Silver Flash" was the 1953 Motor Show exhibit. Lady Docker is pictured here with Osmond Rivers.

Interior of the 1951 "Gold Car".

The 1952 Docker Daimler Special Fixed-Head Coupe.

The interior of the 1955 "Ivory White Golden Zebra Car", with Lady Docker pictured at the wheel.

The "Ivory White Golden Zebra Car".

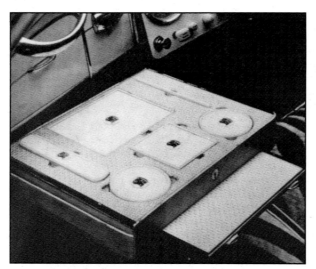

Interior fittings of the "Zebra Car" included a ladies vanity set.

Lady Docker's Daimler dress.

"It was the finest and most costly vehicle in the show, a masterpiece in the old sense of that word, being the means of displaying all the artistry and technique at its creators disposal"

- commented *The Motor*, on the car that came to be known as "Stardust" on account of the side panels being covered with a multitude of stars. Upholstery was in silver silk brocatelle and pale blue crocodile skin covered the panels.

The last and most spectacular of these cars was the "Ivory White Golden Zebra Car", a cornucopia of gold, ivory and real Zebra skin with the body mounted on a Daimler DK400 4 1/2 litre chassis. Gold was again substituted for chrome and as a finishing touch, a solid gold zebra was mounted on the radiator cap. It was, at the time, the most expensive Daimler ever made, costing over £12,000, the price of four substantial three-bedroomed houses in Coventry.

The Dockers were undoubtedly successful at attracting publicity, both as part of Daimler and in their private lives. Although production of all Daimler models was increased through the 1950s, the Dockers ensured that the name became associated with ostentation and extravagance. Despite Lady Docker's ambitions, the cars never did sell to the masses. Lady Docker later recalled:

"No one ever understood what I was doing with these vehicles. In point of fact they were to show the world that we had craftsmen who could build the finest products in the world and that the detailing could be related to the production cars available."

As a direct result of Lady Docker's influence, a completely new model was introduced in May 1953, the Daimler Conquest. Based on a Lanchester Fourteen, this was small by Daimler standards and was intended for the professional and businessman

The Daimler DK400. This example has coachwork by Hooper and was once owned by the Royal Family.

Bernard Docker, pictured in 1945.

Rear view of the Hooper-bodied DK400.

Silverstone 1954. Daimler Conquests featured briefly in a post-war racing programme.

Interior of the Daimler Conquest Century.

The Daimler Conquest Roadster, based on the Conquest saloon, made its debut at the 1953 Motor Show.

who did not want an unduly large and thirsty vehicle. However, it was quite refined for its class and was Daimler's best selling model range throughout the 1950's. This was later modified and renamed the Daimler Conquest Century and a Century-based sports car, the Daimler Roadster, was also introduced.

In 1956, Sir Bernard Docker found himself named as a party in proceedings relating to alleged currency offences and was obliged to resign his appointment at Midland Bank. These allegations were followed by suggestions of mismanagement of the BSA Group.

These allegations were not without foundation. Sir Bernard was found to have been charging his wife's furs and gems in his expenses on the basis that her "glamorous" reputation was an asset to the company. Lady Docker's brother-in-law, R E Smith, unwittingly brought matters to a head on 2nd May 1956, when Sir Bernard proposed his re-election to the Board. The Board was evenly divided over the issue and Sir Bernard, as Chairman was asked to use his casting vote to settle the matter. Convention dictates that a chairman uses a casting vote to defeat a motion so as to maintain the status quo, however, Sir Bernard unwisely voted for the motion and provided his opponents, lead by Jack Sangster, with the opportunity to oust him.

One of BSA's prominent institutional shareholders, the Prudential Assurance Company,

was persuaded by chief accountant John Rowe that the matter was serious enough to warrant removal and Sir Bernard was ousted at a meeting on 31st May. The shareholders ratified this decision on 1st August. Characteristically, the Dockers promptly left and purchased themselves a Rolls-Royce.

Jack Sangster, who had orchestrated the revolt against the Dockers, was appointed Chairman, having previously joined the BSA Board following the sale of his Triumph and Ariel motorcycle firms to the group. A former Triumph colleague, Edward Turner, was appointed head of the newly renamed Automotive Division and was given the formidable task of revamping and rationalising Daimler's range of vehicles. However, this proved to be but a prelude to the eventual sale to Jaguar as Daimler's problems of disorganisation and deficit had resulted in gradual decline.

A number of reasons have been cited for this. Brian Smith, writing in *Royal Daimlers* after interviewing some of the former employees, said:

> *"A considerable number held the opinion that it was a mistaken policy to cater for the middle classes by introducing the Daimler "Fifteen" in the early thirties. They considered that the "well-to-do" with de luxe limousines and lordly laundelettes were aggrieved to find that lesser mortals in the social scale also had a Daimler. Many owners*

Daimler Conquest Shooting Brake. This example was one of six used by ITN as a camera car.

then began to drift to the Crewe product."

This, together with the haphazard provision of spares for the older models certainly resulted in some owners going elsewhere. Another reason suggested is that Daimler failed to keep to the forefront of technological development after the Second World War. Whereas pre-select fluid-flywheel transmission had been an innovation in the 1930s, by the mid-1950s it was an anachronism. Daimlers, always marketed as luxury cars, were not particularly fast or powerful. Nor were they particularly cheap! In trying to appeal to the business and professional market in the 1950s with models such as the Daimler Conquest Century and the Daimler Regency, Daimler was competing with firms such as Jaguar and Rover who were producing broadly similar specifications at lower prices.

Another reason was the domination of the Group by the Docker family over a period of fifty years. There is evidence that Sir Bernard's rise in BSA was stage-managed by his father, Dudley Docker, who treated the group like a small family concern. For example, in 1940, Sir Alexander Roger, chairman of the BSA parent was seconded to the Tank Board. Sir Bernard took over this position whilst also serving as managing director in place of Geoffrey Burton, who had also been seconded, this time to the Ministry of Supply. Burton was never allowed to resume his position having been told in no uncertain terms by the ailing Dudley Docker that he would have to go so as to allow Sir Bernard to be made managing director of the entire group.

Lady Docker's scheme to make Daimler popular very nearly succeeded. Every year at the London Motor Show, the Institute of British Carriage and Automobile Makers organised a coachwork competition and from 1951 to 1955 the Docker Daimlers won either the gold or silver medal. The cars were all later rendered anonymous and sold by the new Board to make capital out of their previous chairman's alleged mismanagement.

Even after leaving BSA, the Dockers remained an eccentric couple who were the subjects of media interest throughout the 1960s.

Sir Bernard Docker died on 22nd May 1978 after a long illness. Lady Norah Docker lingered on for a few years more dying in her sleep on 10th December 1983.

In some way the Docker Daimlers were in advance of their time. In the words of the late Lady Docker:

"All pointed to some model we see today. The Silver Flash and the Zebra Car to the expensive fast luxury coupes like the BMW 633, the others to the Mercedes 600"

In austere post-war Britain of the 1950s, there was no room for such cars.

The 1954 Daimler Regency Sportsman.

Daimler Empress.

A design drawing for the post-war Lanchester LD10 saloon. Note the built-in headlights.

Sales brochure of the Barker-bodied LD10 saloon.

10. THE LAST LANCHESTER

"If the Daimler Motors division of the BSA Group had not then been racked with internal dissensions and on the verge of dissolution, the Sprite may well have been a winner"

Anthony Bird/Francis Hutton-Stott
Lanchester Motor Cars
1964

Following the takeover by Daimler in 1931, Lanchester cars, though very fine automobiles, were very much the poor relation of the Daimlers. There was considerable goodwill attached to the name and both before and after the Second World War, the larger Daimlers were "badge-engineered" as Lanchesters, the most prominent customer being the Duke of York, later King George VI.

Indeed, this practice continued until the late 1940s, with a particularly fine example being built on a Daimler DE27 chassis for the royal house of Nawanagar, who had been buying Lanchesters since the 1920s. This particular car was bought for the use of "Ranji", the famous Indian cricketer.

The Lanchester LD10 was conceived prior to the war, but production commenced in 1946. Originally with a Briggs all-steel body, it was replaced in 1951 by a coachbuilt Barker-bodied car following the takeover at Briggs by Ford. The Lanchester 14 was introduced in 1950, and in 1953, an attempt to move the Lanchester up-market with the introduction of the Lanchester 2.4 litre Dauphins, with coachwork by Hooper, was abandoned after testing only two prototypes. This, together with an aborted convertible coupé of the Lanchester 14, represented several attempts to revive the once-proud Lanchester name, which failed because of a poor pricing policy, dealer resistance and a poor reception by the motoring public.

Daimler made one final attempt to resurrect the Lanchester. The 2 litre Lanchester Leda had been a heavy, underpowered car, and it was decided to try and improve on the original concept. Increasing the engine to 2.5 litres eventually led to the

Lovely to look at – delightful to drive

Swift modern body styling...thoughtful interior planning for roomy comfort ...high speed cruising with exceptional stability...new developments in engineering design...every feature adds up to the superb achievement of the Lanchester Fourteen. It's a car you will enjoy—built in the famous Lanchester tradition.

Independent front suspension. Hydraulic telescopic shock absorbers. Complete suspension system included in the fully automatic chassis lubrication system

the lively...likeable
Lanchester
Fourteen

BY APPOINTMENT
Motor Car Manufacturers
To H.M. King George VI
THE LANCHESTER MOTOR CO. LTD. COVENTRY

The Lanchester Fourteen. Badly underpowered by its two-litre four-cylinder engine, this was the predecessor to the Daimler Conquest which was to be Daimler's best selling car in the 1950s.

The Lanchester New Drophead Coupe was widely advertised but did not go into production.

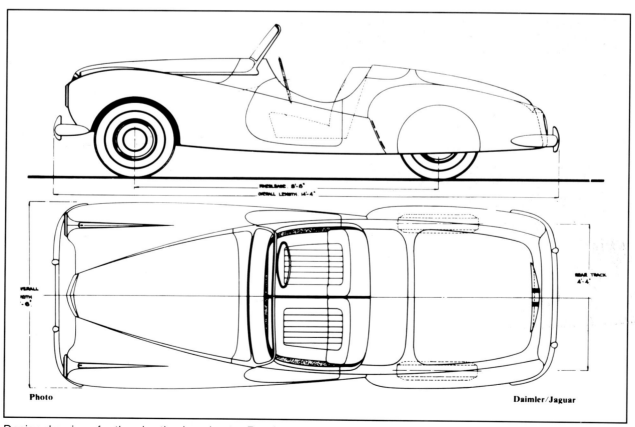

Design drawings for the abortive Lanchester Roadster.

The Lanchester phase one Sprite. This photograph clearly shows the resemblance to the contemporary Hillman Minx.

The only post-war Lanchester Drophead Coupé to go into production. This was one of two built by Abbotts of Farnham.

introduction of the Daimler Conquest range of cars, which were a direct development of the Lanchester Fourteen. A second option was also explored. Daimler wanted to market a light economical vehicle, which meant a radical re-design of the Lanchester. The eventual solution was inspired by a popular French Car which was an unlikely candidate for interest from a luxury car manufacturer. At the instigation of the Chairman, Sir Bernard Docker, an example of this vehicle was assessed.

In the early 1950s Panhard & Levassor had produced a sleek aluminium-bodied car, the Dyna 850. Capable of over 75mph and returning approximately 40 miles per gallon, a small light car of this type would have fitted nicely into the Daimler and Lanchester range, by providing a small economic entry model. The original intention had been to assemble the Dyna 850 in England, but the government precluded that particular option by preventing the import of ready made body panels into the UK. BSA, in spite of its size and resources, did not have the capacity to produce its own such panels. The only solution was to design a completely new Lanchester which incorporated the best features of the Dyna 850.

To cut down the weight of the new vehicle, it was to be of chassisless construction, with strength being derived from the floorpan, transmission tunnel, front cross-member, wheel arches and inner side panels. Engine access was provided by allowing the whole bonnet to swing upwards together with the outer wings. The engine was a four-cylinder derivative of the proven Daimler Conquest engine and a number of non-structural body panels were constructed of light alloy rather than steel.

The last Lanchester, the phase two Sprite.

In addition, a new fully automatic gearbox was to be provided, and the work was entrusted to *Hobbs Transmissions Limited*, under H F Hobbs and his son John.

The Hobbs transmission had had its origins in the Second World War, when it had been designed by the elder Hobbs for use in a personnel carrier. This project was abandoned following the formation of NATO, which introduced other more developed technology, and Hobbs continued with the transmission's development.

The car, code-named LM150, made its debut at the 1954 Motor Show as the Lanchester Sprite. The phase one Sprite was priced at £760 plus tax and although five chassis numbers were allocated only three cars were ever built. None of the cars were registered and all have been lost.

The development of the model continued. Three phase two prototypes were built and one finished in grey over black with red interior trim, was used for handling and fuel consumption tests. The other two cars with cream and red coachwork respectively were both fitted with red interiors and sent to the MIRA test track. The customary 1,000 mile tests had to be done in stages, as the cars shed parts everywhere and suffered from gearbox and torsional rigidity problems.

In contrast to the phase one Sprites, which had resembled the contemporary Singers, the phase two Sprites bore a distinct family resemblance to the Daimler Conquest, utilising a number of common panels, the front and rear windscreens and a number of suspension systems.

Front bench seats were fitted to make the car a full six-seater and in 1955 two Sprites were displayed at the Motor Show, one finished in silver over black and the other in silver over maroon.

Deliveries were scheduled to commence in mid-1956 at a price of £1,230 including tax. Including the original three phase one prototypes, only thirteen of the cars were ever built.

However, production planning and development continued. An SU carburettor was scheduled to replace the Zenith after 500 cars, after 1,000 units a number of steering modifications were to be introduced. Tentative plans were made for the introduction of more powerful engines and even convertibles were envisaged at one stage. A number of cost-cutting measures were implemented, steel replaced aluminium panels, plastic trim replaced leather and the chrome trim on the vehicle was virtually eliminated.

By 1956 a number of potential customers were already awaiting delivery. However, on 31st May 1956, the driving force behind the Sprite range, Sir Bernard Docker, was ousted. The initial start-up and production costs of approximately £500,000 were cited as the reason for dropping the model, but it was clear that the new Board were attempting to distance themselves from the former chairman's projects as quickly as possible.

They continued with the production of the Conquest range, which was the best-selling model by Daimler during the 1950s. Ironically, the Lanchester Sprite would have cost 20% less to produce to roughly the same specification. In fact, the price of the Daimler was reduced to below that anticipated for the Sprite, which undoubtedly contributed to the poor financial performance of the Company in the late 1950s.

The name of Lanchester was finally dropped in Spring 1956, almost sixty years after the first Lanchester had taken to the road.

11. Daimler by Jaguar

"A manufacturer cannot be far off the mark when it is the ambition of every keen motorist to own one of his cars."

Sir William Lyons

Born in Blackpool in 1901, William Lyons was educated at the local grammar school, later reading engineering at Manchester Technical College. He then worked for the firm of Crossley and at this time met William Walmsley, who had begun making motorcycle sidecars in his front room assisted by his wife, who made the upholstery.

On 4th September 1922, with a capital of £1,000, a lease to the top two floors of an old building in Blackpool and a good deal of youthful enthusiasm, the two young motorcycle afficionados went into the business of building motorcycle sidecars, setting up the *Swallow Sidecar Company*.

With a combination of acute business sense and a flair for design, one of these enthusiasts, William Lyons, established a quality sidecar in a very short time. Within a year the Company had acquired its own stand at the Motor Cycle Show with their sidecars being displayed at the stands of four other

William Lyons.

motorcycle manufacturers. Soon afterwards two further factory sites were acquired to cope with the expanding sidecar business, with yet more space being acquired in mid-1926, Lyons' Swallow Coachbuilding Company went into the motor car business.

The first Austin-based Swallow appeared in 1926. Based on the Austin Seven, the Swallow had a more attractive and luxurious body than the basic car. In May 1927, this car was announced to the public and was followed three months later by the Morris Cowley Swallow.

By the following year the newly renamed *Swallow Sidecar and Coachbuilding Company* was bursting at the seams with Austin Seven chassis, having taken an order for 500 Austin Swallows from Henlys. The premises were again relocated to Foleshill, Coventry, and the Company continued to expand adding a Wolseley Hornet Swallow to its range in 1931 and a Swallow-bodied Standard Sixteen.

Added by an ingenious line in advertising "If you cannot buy a Rolls you can buy distinction" Lyons was on to a winner, offering a compact luxury car which was exceptional value for money.

In October 1931, with introduction of the SS1, Lyons established a marque in its own right. Supplied with a chassis by Standard to Lyons' specification, the SS1 was a full four-seater saloon with a sliding roof, a comprehensive range of equipment and endowed with a graceful and distinctive body style. *The Autocar* later described it as *"long, low and rakishly sporting, the general effect being that of a powerful sports coupe costing £1,000, although the actual price is less than a third of that figure"*. Later the saloon was joined by a "miniature", the SSII. The two cars were priced at just £310 and £210 respectively and had all the ingredients of what was to be the Lyons secret of success; good looks, outstanding performance and remarkable value for money.

Announcing the SS Jaguar on 24th September 1936 re-emphasised the SS price concept. Elegant and well-proportioned, the four door saloon was fast, luxurious and outstanding value-for-money at £395.

Four examples of the Lyons style. The first is a Standard-Swallow from circa 1929, the second is an SS1. Opposite, the SS100 and Mark V Jaguar.

Floated as a public company in 1935, *SS Cars Limited* gradually increased its range, catering for a booming export market and soon enjoying a reputation for competition success as well as for value. With the advent of the Second World War, the Company's activities switched to aircraft component manufacturing.

In March 1945, following the exposure of the atrocities carried out in wartime Germany by Hitler's SS troops, the name SS was dropped and *Jaguar Cars Limited* began to resume production of motor cars, up-dating the pre-war models for Britain's export drive.

September 1948 saw the introduction of the Jaguar Mark V, first in a new programme which later that year introduced the Jaguar XK120, powered by the new XK six-cylinder 3 1/2 litre power unit, an engine which remains in production (albeit in 4.2 litre form) to this day.

Meantime development continued on an all new saloon, the Jaguar Mark VII. Again, distinctive styling, 100mph performance and a modest purchase price brought success both at home and abroad, particularly in the United States where ownership of a British Jaguar became fashionable in the 1950s. Entry in to the competition world as

The development of the last all-Daimler sports car, the SP250. The prototype is pictured here on test in Wales, whilst below is another prototype with fins to the rear, and an air intake built into the bonnet.

A styling exercise for the Hooper-bodied close-coupled Coupe,

an official team in 1951 led to a series of victories until 1957, when the official team withdrew.

A monocoque compact was introduced in 1955, later updated in 1959 to become the Jaguar Mark II, described as "..the businessman's express...an outstandingly beautiful car that clearly established Jaguar as a class leader in terms of value for money performance, state of the art handling, high quality interior appointments and distinctive exterior styling."

Lyons' "Grace, Pace and Space" was the order of the day, and this impressive ability to undercut all his rivals with a pricing policy which put his cars well within the reach of the business and professional motorist was the secret of his continued success as other, more established companies went into decline. In contrast to Daimler, Jaguar used innovations gleaned from an intense racing and development programme, so the motorist was always offered outstanding performance for his money. Whereas Daimler had offered a bewildering variety of chassis types and production models,

Lyons offered a small sports and saloon car range which found and exploited a profitable niche in the market. It is also worth noting that Lyons took the time and trouble to develop a market in the United States, whereas Daimler relied on a shrinking empire for its export sales.

Whilst Daimler lost money and direction towards the end of the 1950s, Jaguar expanded. During 1951 and 1952 Jaguar moved into Daimler's former Browns Lane works, a one million square feet factory site, where the company remains to this day. By the end of the 1950s, continuing success once again was putting pressure on factory space, but a government moratorium prevented expansion into new land in the Coventry area.

In 1960 BSA made it known that they wished to dispose of Daimler. Jaguar was by then "bursting at the seams". The then BSA chairman, Jack Sangster, entered into preliminary negotiations with Lyons to sell the entire share capital and assets of Daimler, which at the time included the Coventry Radford works, barely two miles from Brown's Lane.

The production Daimler SP250.

The Ogle-bodied Daimler SX250 was built by David Ogle in 1962, but never went into production because of Ogle's death.

Daimler SP250s enjoyed some racing successes, particularly in the USA. Here, Duncan Black puts the SP through its paces.

The price was finally agreed at £3,400,000. Lyons recalled in 1969:

"I cannot recall a more amicable deal with anyone, although when we both thought everything had been settled, a matter of £10,000 arose between us. (Some pensions matter had been left out of the negotiations). Since each of us was honestly convinced that this was in our own favour, we decided that the only way to settle the matter was to toss-up for it. I am pleased to say that I won."

The acquisition provided Jaguar with an additional one million square feet of floor space, a prestigious range of cars, buses and armoured vehicles and a large quantity of new plant, bought to manufacture the newly developed range of V8 engines. The era of "Daimler by Jaguar" was about to begin.

In 1960, one of the most valuable of the newly acquired Daimler assets was the recently developed Turner V8 engine. An advanced design, deriving much from Turner's experience as a motor cycle engineer, it was tested on both the prototype Daimler SP250 Sports Car and in a Daimler Conquest Saloon in 1958. The Company had high hopes for the new engine and the release of a new 2 1/2 litre saloon was eagerly awaited by both press and public. Styling exercises were carried out on a Vauxhall Cresta bodyshell, but the 2 1/2 litre V8 was never released by Daimler under BSA.

A larger V8 of 4561cc was taken to the production stage and the Daimler Majestic Major, a large luxury saloon was released at the London Motor Show in 1959 together with the Daimler SP250, a small sports car with a fibreglass body.

The Daimler SP250 production line.

One of the remarkable features of the V8 engine was its incredibly smooth and near silent running at almost any speed. The 4 1/2 litre unit in particular was capable of taking the 36.5cwt Daimler Majestic Major to speeds in excess of 120mph. The smaller 2 1/2 litre V8 in the Daimler SP250 was capable of similar speeds and Jaguar lost no time in assessing the potential of both engines.

During the early stages of the Jaguar Mark X development programme a 4 1/2 litre V8 was fitted to a Mark X bodyshell. This prototype improved the 0-100 time of the vehicle by 6 seconds and was capable of sustaining speeds of 133-134 mph. However the Jaguar Mark X was fitted with a six-cylinder 3.8 litre XK unit when finally released.

The lighter 2 1/2 litre unit was tested in the compact Jaguar (Mark I) bodyshell. Differing from the Jaguar XK engine in three respects, being smaller, lighter and providing stronger engine braking throughout the gear ranges, the V8 was shoehorned into the Jaguar Mark II bodyshell and fitted with type 35 Borg-Warner transmission. The

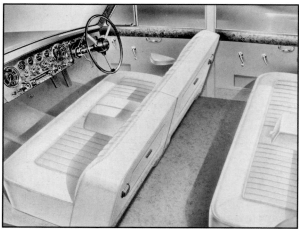

The Daimler Majestic was introduced at the 1958 Motor Show, and was followed by the Majestic Major in 1959. The Majestic Major was powered by Edward Turner's 4 1/2 litre V8 engine, and was capable of speeds of up to 120mph. The interior was particularly spacious.

new Daimler 2 1/2 litre V8 was released in October 1962. Although no real match in performance terms to the 3.4 and 3.8 Jaguar Mark II's, the new Daimler had better acceleration and was faster than the Jaguar 2.4.

Daimler had intended to release a closed sports coupé with Hooper bodywork. However this was not ready for production by 1960 and was dropped by Jaguar, who were by then preparing their own sports coupé, the Jaguar E-Type.

Although a number of modifications were made to the V8 range, Jaguar's development costs were increasing at an alarming rate. For example £250,000 had to be spent in 1967 to modify the Jaguar E-Type to comply with United States safety and exhaust emission requirements. As cars became more sophisticated and were subjected to more complex legislation, it became clear that a diverse range of vehicles using differing components was unsustainable.

The Daimler Majestic Major limousine. This example belonged to English China Clays.

The 1960s was the decade of "badge-engineering" when cars of the same basic specification were released with differing marque badges in order to appeal to a variety of markets. Badge-engineering was an often vain attempt to retain customers of the smaller firms which were being absorbed in the rush of take-overs, mergers and amalgamations. By using the same basic specification and distinguishing margins, the new conglomerates were able, for a short time, to retain some of the customers of former manufacturers without incurring the costs of maintaining a separate and distinct production line.

The V8s were undoubtedly finely engineered power plants, but low volume production of the Daimler SP250, the Daimler Majestic Major and its Limousine derivative must have been an uneconomic use of factory floor space and the plant. The Daimler SP250 was a fine sports car, but something of an oddball which never sold as well as the Jaguar E-Type and the small Daimler was phased out in 1964.

The Daimler Majestic Major lingered on until discontinued in 1968, when only five cars per week were being produced. The 2 ¹/₂ litre range, however, was updated in 1967 to become the top-of-the-range option of the Jaguar Mark II based cars, but production of this model was phased out in 1969.

Gradually, over nine years the Daimler engineering was phased out of the Jaguar-Daimler range. A "new" Daimler, a Jaguar 420-based badge-engineering exercise, the Daimler Sovereign, first appeared in 1966, with Jaguar XK engine becoming the new "Daimler" power plant.

Whereas famous names such as Riley and Wolseley eventually disappeared, Lyons was not

Right:
The 2¹/₂ litre saloon was originally intended by Daimler to be based around the Vauxhall Cresta bodyshell. No examples were built, but the above styling exercise and the design drawing shown here clearly indicate what the car may have looked like. Following the takeover by Jaguar in 1960, the Turner engine was married to a Borg-Warner Type 35 Automatic gearbox and "shoe-horned" into a Jaguar Mark II bodyshell. William Lyons preferred to use this bodyshell and the result was this stylish compact saloon, introduced in 1962.

slow in realising the tremendous potential that was attached to the name "Daimler". Although Jaguars were fine cars, they were perceived as suffering from one fundamental defect. Ken Clayton, in *Jaguar, Rebirth of a Legend* in 1988 explained that:

> *"..attractive as the Company's cars were, they tended to be seen as too racy for the establishment. A Jaguar was not quite respectable, even in the 1960s. In those days a sales manager might have one, but it was definitely not an acceptable car for a Finance Director. Film makers recognised the Mark II saloon as a superb getaway car for bank robbers and underworld hoodlums. Every crime film of the time seems to have involved a chase with the villains racing away in their Mark II, usually to crash it in a spectacular fashion. The image did not help sales. One man who joined the Board of a big company in*

> *the mid-60s recalls that when he was appointed, no director had a Jaguar."*

By contrast, the name Daimler had an air of staid respectability about it. Daimler meant establishment. Daimler had been for most of the century the Royal carriage. Whilst the salesmen drove a Jaguar, the directors drove a Daimler.

By fitting a Daimler engine in the Jaguar bodyshell with the 2 $^1/_2$ litre V8, Lyons was appealing to the establishment with a very clever marketing ploy which still has merit to this day. The 1966 Daimler Sovereign capitalised on that perception of the Daimler name and retained a market which Jaguar would have had tremendous difficulty in penetrating on its own in Britain and the Commonwealth. However, because of the neglect of the United States market in the crucial post-war years (and previously), Daimler never had any impact on the other side of the Atlantic, where the association remains with Daimler-Benz, manufacturers of the Mercedes range of cars.

The 2$^{1}/_{2}$ litre V8 proved popular and Sir Richard Attenborough was one of several celebrity owners. Here he is pictured at the Patrick Collection in Birmingham handing over the keys and registration documents.

The Daimler V8-250 was an updated saloon with a number of modifications to the body and interior. Production was phased out in 1969. This car is owned by the author and has been in regular use for over twenty years.

1966 Jaguar publicity photo of the new Daimler Sovereign. This was in most respects a Jaguar 420, but with a more luxurious interior and Daimler grille and badges.

12. TAKE-OVER, INDEPENDENCE, TAKE-OVER

"By the time Lyons sold it, Jaguar had relied for too long on minimal investment and inadequate management to be viable in the long term."

Ken Clayton
Jaguar, Rebirth of a Legend
1988

In the mid-1960s, Jaguar was a prime target for takeover. BMC recognised that the Jaguar and Daimler ranges were far more successful than their own Vanden Plas Princess 4 litre R and Austin-Healey's in the luxury and sports car market and courted Lyons for several years before he agreed to the merger. The takeover fever of the 60s was the British Motor Industry's attempt to form a conglomerate large enough to compete with Ford and Chrysler, who were acquiring a larger market share in Britain through their own take-over programme.

Thirty-one independent British motor manufacturers exhibited at the 1948 Earls Court Show. In the following twenty years many failed for a variety of reasons or were taken over by other, more acquisition-hungry groups. One of the reasons for this demise of the independents was that technological advance in the post-war years and into the 1960s made it virtually impossible for a smallish independent manufacturer to compete on the same

terms with the large American and European firms. As technical advances became more refined and complex, the pre-production costs became prohibitive and many manufacturers lacked the financial resources to maintain the competitive edge over the larger conglomerates. The result was a gradual erosion of market share and volumes with overseas manufacturers beginning to satisfy consumer demand in the shape of keenly priced imports.

With the conivance of the then Labour government, the British Leyland Motor Corporation was formed with the aim of providing a UK-based motor manufacturing base which would be large enough to compete on equal terms with the Americans and the Europeans. Although the actual legal structure necessary for this operation was put in place relatively quickly, management structures were haphazard and communication breakdowns and incompetence were rife throughout. The original aim had been to produce a rationalised

Front three-quarter view of the Daimler Sovereign. The most obvious difference is the treatment of the Daimler grille.

Interior of the 420 Sovereign. Wider pleats in the leather and the Daimler "D" distinguish it from the Jaguar.

The Jaguar XK 4.2 straight-six engine in a Daimler Sovereign "420".

model range, with finer engines and bodyshells with combined resources being capable of making quantum leaps in the development of motoring technology.

Whilst Ford and Chrysler had several decades to perfect their operational and management structure, British Leyland Motor Holdings in the late 1960s was at best a loose amalgamation of several independent companies, with complicated dealer networks, model ranges and parts operations. Different parts of the so-called management "team" had little in common except a common background in the motor industry. This resulted in a weak management riddled with inconsistencies, which in the long term analysis, simply failed to put the structures in place necessary for the achievement of the conglomerate's aims.

Ironically the very failure to install strong management resulted in Jaguar retaining some semblance of operational independence and a distinct identity, compared with Austin, Morris, Rover and Standard-Triumph, who were all eventually and painfully integrated into the larger structure. Research and development continued separately and with the connivance of the design team, the programme of styling on the XJ40 project was quite deliberately aimed at retaining the Jaguar six-cylinder engines with a design that conspired to exclude the ubiquitous Rover V8 engine.

In October 1966, three months after the takeover by BMC, the first Daimler Sovereign was introduced. Under the bonnet was the 4235cc XK engine used in the Jaguar 420G and Jaguar E-Type. The car was lavishly equipped with leather and walnut very much in evidence. The "badge-engineering" of the marque continued in 1969 with the introduction of a new Daimler Sovereign, which was to a very similar specification to the Jaguar XJ6. Again the vehicle was provided with slightly more lavish appointments, but this time a 2.8 litre engine was offered as well as the 4.2.

By 1972, a long wheelbase Sovereign was added to the range, aimed at and ideally suited to the chauffeur-driven executive and was drawn from the tradition of cars of an earlier era. On 11th July 1972 a further effort was made to draw on past glories with the introduction of the Daimler Double-Six. The then Chairman, F R W "Lofty" England remarked:

"As a Daimler apprentice during its heyday I well remember the original Double-Six being renowned for its silence and smoothness. As these are amongst the most outstanding characteristics of the 12 cylinder Daimler,... we had no difficulty in deciding to re-adopt the famous name."

1969 saw the introduction of the Daimler Sovereign based on the Jaguar XJ6. Again, this was essentially an exercise in badge engineering. However a 2.8 litre Jaguar XK engine was offered with the Daimler, though this resulted in an underpowered car.

On 26th September 1972, an exclusive version of the long wheelbase Daimler Double Six was released. As the ultimate Daimler of the 1970s, the Daimler Double-Six Vanden Plas drew comparisons with the Rolls-Royce Silver Shadow. Stanley Sedgewick wrote in The Autocar:

"The drive (in the Daimler) served to confirm my opinion that the 12 cylinder Daimler is the best value for money in the world."

The Jaguar XJ and Daimler Sovereign series of cars were continually upgraded throughout the 1970s and 1980s. Further improvements to the specification and appointments were made with the introduction of the Series II cars in 1973. Amongst these was an exclusive Daimler Double-Six Coupe. Further improvements were made to the four-door saloons, but on the introduction of the Series III Daimler Sovereigns, Vanden Plas' and Double-Sixes, the Coupe was dropped.

In April 1987, the last XK-engined Daimler Sovereigns were produced and the assembly-line was turned over to production of the new "XJ40" Jaguar XJ6, Jaguar Sovereign and Daimler after a development period of over fourteen years. Ironically, the decision in the early 1970s to design a bodyshell which precluded the installation of a "V" engine meant that the Jaguar V12 and Daimler Double-Six are still the top of the range cars in a XJ6 Series III bodyshell that has now been in continuous production for 11 years. Plans are for a new V12 to be made, but no release date had been fixed at the time of writing.

Daimler was best known for its elegant limousines that wafted the Nobility and Royalty to official engagements. The Daimler Majestic Major Limousine (derived from the 4 1/2 litre Daimler Majestic Major saloon) was by the mid-1960s decidedly old fashioned. Following the take-over of Jaguar by BMC in July 1966, the decision was taken to develop a new limousine.

Vanden Plas (England) 1923 Limited had for many years produced the Austin Princess limousine, and had been making tentative plans for a replacement before the Jaguar takeover by BMC. Daimler and Vanden Plas were later given responsibility for the development of the all-new limousine.

Of chassisless construction, and utilising many body components from the Jaguar 420 saloon, the new Daimler DS420 Limousine was a radical departure from the previous practice of both Daimler and Vanden Plas. In addition, Jaguar's race-bred all-round independent suspension provided excellent

In 1972 the introduction of the Daimler Double-Six placed Daimler back in the luxury car class with favourable comparisons being drawn with the more expensive Rolls-Royce Silver Shadow.

Jaguar/Daimler production line. The bodyshells are the Series II Jaguar XJ6/Daimler Sovereign.

1974 Daimler Sovereign. The main differences are in the treatment of the front bumper and sidelight assemblies. The interior was considerably upgraded with the introduction of a new dash and seats.

Produced in limited numbers, the Daimler 4.2 Vanden Plas was a styling exercise with one of the most luxurious interiors of any car of the mid-1970s. These cars featured air-conditioning, a high-quality stereo, pleated leather seats and extra walnut trim on the doors.

ride and handling characteristics which proved popular with passengers and drivers alike.

A number of minor modifications were made in 1971 and 1972, and the Limousine underwent a major facelift in 1979.

From its introduction in April 1968 to the present day, the Daimler DS420 has found favour with several royal houses and civic dignatories, in particular with Her Majesty Queen Elizabeth, The Queen Mother, who ordered a new Daimler Limousine in 1970. Since then the Limousine works have been favoured with regular orders from the Royal Mews and the Daimler Company still holds a Royal Warrant. A particularly attractive Landaulette version has been exported to, amongst others, the Governor of Jamaica and the hearse continues to be supplied to the funeral trade.

However, this last of the Daimler Limousines is due to be phased out in 1992 or 1993, following the introduction of a number of new regulations in the single European market. At the time of writing, a successor had not been announced.

A Daimler has not been marketed as a sports car since the demise of the Daimler SP250 in 1964. However, with the improving sales of the Jaguar XJS in the early 1980s, a design exercise was carried out on the Jaguar XJS, with a view to marketing it as a Daimler. The result was a rather graceful Grand

Tourer with a number of detailed changes to the chrome trim, including the addition of a crinkled radiator, reminiscent of the last of the Daimler SP250s. The rear window panels were reworked with a new screen and overall the effect was that of quite subtle refinement on a set of already fine lines. Unfortunately, the exercise was never seen through to production, although the prototype is still at Browns Lane. The prospects of the Daimler name ever gracing a sports coupé are now greatly diminished, with resources concentrated on refining the XJ6 saloons.

Sir William Lyons had considerable doubts about Jaguar's ability to retain any distinct identity within the British Leyland conglomerate.

Prior to the take-over by BMC, Jaguar had made profits during every year since its formation. Although the position during the 1970s was not very clear, being inextricably bound up in British Leyland, it is thought that the Company was probably making a modest profit every year until 1979, when losses accumulated over that and the following two years. This appeared to have happened despite, rather than because of British Leyland. Although Lyons' chairmanship was succeeded by former Daimler apprentice Lofty England, Donald Stokes insisted that Geoffrey Robinson be brought in as Managing Director in 1973. Fortunately for the Company,

The current Daimler Double Six. Although the Daimler Sovereign Series III was phased out following the introduction of the Jaguar "XJ40" (new XJ6), the Series III bodyshell continued to house the 12-cylinder engine. Because of internal rivalries during the XJ40 project, the new bodyshell was deliberatly designed not to take a V-engine.

Interior of the current Daimler Double-Six.

The Daimler DS420 Limousine. Introduced to replace the ageing and dated Daimler Majestic Major Limousine, the above vehicle is shown during testing at Silverstone.

This Daimler DS420 Landaulette was specially made for the Governor of Jamaica.

The Daimler Executive Limousine. Built as a one-off by Jaguar, the interior featured car-phone, facsimile machine and on-board computer.

Robinson was an able executive who worked closely with England in planning for expansion. Shortly after his arrival, Robinson announced a £60-million investment programme intended to raise combined production of Jaguars and Daimlers to 60,000 cars per year. The Ryder Report, long since discredited, concluded that Jaguar should lose its separate identity and become a division of BL. This resulted in the Board being disbanded and management being dispersed around the Browns Lane and Radford plants under separate control.

Declining morale resulted in productivity and standards dropping. For example, sales of 32,589 cars in 1971 declined to under 23,000 in 1972, increased sharply to 30,000 in 1974 and then went into gradual decline, 14,353 being sold in 1981.

Problems with new plant, quality control and a constricting export market caused by the relative strength of Sterling after the 1979 General Election all contributed to a malaise which prompted drastic action in 1980.

As part of a programme of rationalisation, the labour force was reduced by a third and improvements in productivity resulted in output per man doubling in the subsequent two years.

1981 saw a gradual return to profitability, with a weaker pound, better quality control and improved productivity. Management was strengthened with the setting up of a Treasury department to control and hedge the Company's vulnerability to the currency markets and a new system of "just-in-time" stock control was introduced. With the re-election of the Conservative government in 1983, pressure was applied by the Department of Trade and Industry to British Leyland to float one of its operations as an independent publically quoted company. At first it was widely thought that Land-Rover would be floated, but poor results in the early 1980s resulted in attention being switched to Jaguar. Jaguar, having retained a measure of operational independence during the years following the BMC takeover had, as part of the Jaguar-Rover-Triumph division of British Leyland, been examined as a candidate for privatisation several times. In December 1984, Norman Lamont, then Minister of State for Industry announced that Jaguar would be privatised the following year.

In the previous two years, Jaguar had been courted by Ford, who suggested that they act as distributors and dealers in West Germany and North America. Although no takeover appears to have been envisaged at this stage, it was suggested that Jaguar produce a car for distribution through the Ford outlets. A Daimler was suggested, but the obvious confusion with Daimler-Benz would have created problems in West Germany in particular. Although Lanchester was suggested, confusion with Lancaster, established by thorough market research, eventually resulted in the whole scheme being dropped.

This styling exercise on the Jaguar XJS suggests what a Daimler version of this vehicle may have looked like. The main differences are in the treatment of the Daimler grille and the re-styling of the rear screen.

Ford was later followed by BMW and by General Motors. BMW entered into discussions about a collaboration on a compact Jaguar, loosely based around the then BMW 5-series floorpan, but despite lengthy discussions nothing emerged other than disclosure of each company's future plans. General Motors, like Ford, were seeking a prestige manufacturer to add to its stable, but again, lengthy discussions came to nothing.

With Jaguar's return to profitability under the management of John Egan's team, British Leyland was understandably reluctant to privatise almost immediately, having financed the heavy losses of the early 1980s. However, the matter was finally resolved when the government took the decision that upon flotation British Leyland would relinquish all control in Jaguar and that the government would retain a "golden share" until December 31st 1990 to protect the newly floated company from immediate takeover.

Preparations continued and an offer for sale was made on 2nd July with a final date for applications to be in by August 3rd. On 6th August the announcement was made that the offer had been over-subscribed by 8.3 times at 165 pence per share. In the first day of trading following the flotation approximately 25% of the issued capital of 178 million shares changed hands.

With the return of Jaguar to independence, continued existence of the Daimler marque appeared to be assured. On 23rd March 1983, the Jaguar-Daimler Heritage Trust had been formed jointly by Jaguar Cars Limited and the British Motor Industry Heritage Trust as a subsidiary of Jaguar Cars Limited. Following privatisation, the trust continued to be active and a small museum was set up at the Browns Lane factory reception. Committed to the preservation of Daimler cars for the nation, the trust acquired a number of distinctive and important cars including at least one Royal Daimler, discovered in Australia and re-imported in 1988.

Dependence on overseas markets like the United States had an adverse affect on Jaguar's profits during 1988, the Company being exposed to the uncertainties of fluctuating exchange rates. The continued strength of Sterling against the dollar in 1988, when the Company had sold forward the majority of its dollar receivables resulted in the value of US sales falling despite record production levels of 51,939 vehicles and sales of 50,603 vehicles. Although an adverse exchange rate had been anticipated in 1988, the company had been unable to mitigate against this with increased productivity and sales. To add to its troubles, the United States market softened, with the effect that pricing action was curtailed and market share fell. Nevertheless, Jaguar's performance was creditable and they fared better than competitors such as Porsche.

Although the Company continued with its

The current Daimler saloon.

development programme, high capital expenditure and rising interest rates brought high depreciation and financing costs. This placed further pressure on management to squeeze margins and increase profitability. Unfortunately, one of the results of this was the troublesome industrial disputes throughout 1989. This was reflected in the share price of the recently floated company, which began to fall.

At the same time negotiations with both Ford and General Motors recommenced. Although at first this was perceived as talks with a view to possible joint ventures, rumours of an impending take-over by Ford were fuelled by the purchases of shares and stakebuilding by Ford. Speculation about the government's "golden share" continued. An announcement by Nicholas Ridley that the government would relinquish its golden share prior to the original deadline of 31st December 1990 virtually cleared the way for a bid, despite provisions in the Company's articles which forbade shareholdings in excess of 15% of the share capital.

A shareholders meeting was convened for 1st December. This was to be the last to be held by an independent Jaguar Plc and a series of resolutions allowed an agreed bid by Ford to acquire the Company's shares. That day Jaguar was officially notified that the government would not oppose such

a transaction and that the acquisition would not be referred to the Monopolies and Mergers Commission. By 8th December, Ford was able to announce that it had received valid acceptances of its offer accounting for over 77% of the Jaguar shares. By 22nd December, this had increased to the 90% required to allow the compulsory purchase of all of the issued shares.

The announcement in January of further falls in Jaguar's sales figures came together with Ford's appointments to the new Jaguar Board. Despite falls in sales overall, there was an increase in sales of the Daimler Limousine from 154 to 194, with first quarter sales in 1990 later totalling 54 vehicles.

On February 5th, Sir John Egan vacated the Chief Executive's office at Jaguar and Bill Hayden, a senior Ford executive, moved in. Later, on March 27th, it was announced that Sir John Egan would retire from Jaguar at the end of June.

The speed of the takeover took many by surprise, although the commercial justification was quite obvious. Jaguar as an independent, though a profitable concern, was vulnerable in a number of areas. Dependence on overseas markets, despite hedging against exchange rate movements, resulted in alarming effects on profits when local markets became more competitive. In the United States

Originally powered by a Jaguar 3.6 litre AJ6 engine, this was upgraded to 4 litres in 1989.

The interior is the traditional Daimler walnut and leather combination.

Daimler never made any impact in the United States. The use of the Daimler name there is associated with Daimler-Benz. However, the Majestic was briefly reincarnated in 1989 as a limited edition top-of-the-range model for the US markets, the Jaguar Vanden Plas Majestic.

The current Daimler DS420 facility. Here the workforce is shown with a Daimler DS420 delivered to the Royal Household in summer1988.

particularly, competitive pricing together with the comparative weakness of the dollar, affected the results of many European manufacturers. Those most able to ride out the storm were the volume luxury car makers such as Mercedes and BMW. In addition high development costs were a severe drain on the Company's resources. Ford, it was argued, had the financial clout and technical expertise for Jaguar to draw upon in lean times. In turn, Ford added a prestige car to its stable, which enabled it to penetrate the luxury car and sports car market.

One of the mistaken, though surprisingly widely held beliefs was that the distinct Jaguar and Daimler marques would be replaced by badge engineering on up-market Ford saloons. This was errant nonsense. Not only did it conflict with Ford's stated policy, but it made no commercial sense to eliminate one of the key selling factors of Jaguars and Daimlers, their exclusivity. Indeed, an earlier acquisition, that of Aston Martin, resulted in few changes to model specifications and the cars' development as a distinct marque. *The Times* commented as follows:

> "It would be no exaggeration to say that senior Ford management, in Detroit as well as Brentwood, Essex, is verging on the neurotic about its wish for Jaguar to remain de principio as well as de facto quite autonomous and independent of its parent company.

> This extends to the strict understanding that Ford executives may visit Brown's Lane only when invited to do so. Dropping in to visit the Coventry factory is not only discouraged - it is not even allowed."

Ford's resources have been allocated to provide at least £1 billion investment into Jaguar and Daimler. This alleviates a problem that had dogged both companies, as well as Lanchester, during the entirety of their respective existences, virtually living hand-to-mouth through lack of adequate working capital. The inability to plan a coherent long-term strategy had made them more vulnerable to fluctuating market forces than Ford ever was, except in perhaps the very early days of its existence. The result of this was over-dependence on the successful flavour-of-the-month as opposed to a continuous upgrading and replacement programme.

If Ford carries out its stated intentions, new Jaguar and Daimler models will be appearing in the next five to ten years. Smaller sized luxury cars are being planned, with the intention of finding a niche market. Production is planned to rise from 50,000 to 200,000 cars per year.

The commitment to Daimler remains at the highest level. It is likely that the marque will be given a more distinct identity in the future, as Daimler operates in a slightly different market from Jaguar. The future, therefore, seems assured.

We shall wait and see.

Appendix I
Daimler and Lanchester chassis types 1936-1990

Many of the Daimler records for pre-war chassis types were lost in the bombings of Coventry of 1940 and 1941. However, the records from 1945 are reasonably complete, although much was lost during the period when Jaguar was under the control of British Leyland.

Generally - "L" represented Lanchester, "D" represented Daimler.

LA14
LA14-1
30,000-33099:
33,100-33,418
LA14-2
33,425-35,024
LA14-3
35,025-35,124
LA14-1
Refers to the Lanchester exhibited at the London Motor Show in 1936 and released to the public in 1936, 1937 and 1938. Commonly known as the Lanchester Roadrider.
LA14-2
Refers to the Lanchester Roadrider De Luxe introduced in 1937. This utilised the same chassis as the Daimler Fifteen, which was otherwise quite distinct from the Lanchester Roadrider. Body options were four-and six-light saloons, the four-lights often known as the Sports or Sportsman models.

DB17
DB17-1
44,500-45,499
DB17-2
48,550-49,049
The designation DB17 applied to the 1937 season 2166cc Daimlers, which succeeded the Daimler Fifteen.
DB17-2 Cars had independent front suspension, introduced in 1938.

DB18
DB18-1
45,050-49,549
56,000-56,135
2 1/2 litre saloons and foursome coupes:
50,013-50,031;
50,040-51039;
51,800-52,799;
53,000-53,749;
53,000-53,749;

54,500-54,949;
56,000-56,135.
Daimler Consort:
55,000-55,999;
56,200-56,699;
57,010-59,009;
59,240-59,989
Daimler Special Sports:
53,750-53,999;
56,136-56,188;
56,700-56,774;
59,010-59,239

Lanchester Roadrider.

This model was introduced in 1939, upgrading the Daimler Fifteen with a 2,522cc, 18.02HP. Four and six-light saloons were standard. £90 extra could buy the Daimler Ritz. The Daimler Dolphin was the softtop version of this model.

Post-war, this model designation continued, although it was often referred to as the 2 1/2 litre saloon. Barker and Hooper built a number of four-seater tourers, the Barker cars being known as the Special Sports Coupé, based on the pre-war Dolphin.

The Daimler DB18 Consort, introduced in 1949, was a development of the pre-war car that made certain changes to the bodyline, including the introduction of built in headlights.

Daimler DB18 , as used by Winston Churchill.

Hooper- Bodied Daimler Ambulance.

DC24

Probably a replacement for the Daimler Light Twenty and Daimler Light Straight Eight, this car did not go into production.

DC27

54,000-54,499

This was the Ambulance version of the Daimler DE27 Limousine. Both Barker and Hooper built bodies for the Ambulance.

LD10

60,000-60,024
60,025-61,024
61,800-63,225
63,226-63,804

Daimler Consort Saloon.

Lanchester LD10 with bodywork by Briggs.

A pre-war prototype of the Lanchester LD10 was made but the car did not go into production until April 1946. Two batches had Briggs coachwork, but from the third batch, Barker coachwork was used until the end of the production run in June 1951.

Mock-up for the Daimler DF300 Regency Mark I.

Lanchester LD10 with bodywork by Barker.

DF300/1
Prototype; 57,000-57,009
80,000-80,007
The numbered designation is changed indicating cc and left or right hand drive, odd numbers being left hand and even numbers right hand.
The DF300 was the Daimler Regency, introduced in 1950, with a 3 litre engine. Very few appear to have been built. Saloons look like the Daimler Conquest, but the headlamp assemblies resemble the Daimler Consort.

DE27
D50,000-D 50,005;
D51,040-D51,133:
D51,250-D51,354
This was a 4 litre engined Limousine with a wheelbase of 11'6" utilising the engine developed for the Daimler Armoured Car.

DE36
D50,006-D50,011;
D51,150-D51,243;
D51,700-D51,749;
D51,750-D51,759 (LHD);
D52,800-D52,855.
This was the 5.3 litre Straight Eight engined version of the Daimler DE27, with a wheelbase of 12'3".

Daimler Empress Mark II.

DF250
88,100-88,179
Although the numbers were assigned, no vehicles were ever built. Bob Whyte in *The Daimler and Lanchester Owners Companion* speculates that there may have been a Daimler Regency chassis series, possibly with a Daimler Conquest engine.

DF302/3
82,000-82,027
82,400-82,404
Introduced in 1952 as a convertible built by Barker and later Hooper produced as the Mark II Daimler Empress. Originally powered by a 2 1/2 litre engine, these cars were later given 3 1/2 litre engines.

128

Daimler Regency Mark II.

DF308/9

91,475-91,507

Introduced in 1954, the Daimler Regency Sportsman is easily recognised from the wrap around rear window. A number of Daimler Empress Mark IIIs were also built on this chassis.

DF310/1

88,700-89,057:
90,000-90,016 (Daimler One-O-Four)
96,850-96,898 (Lady's Model)

Known as the Daimler One-O-Four, this car appeared in 1955, the One-O-Four designation arising from test results when the test vehicle achieved 104mph. The Ladies model was of broadly similar specification, but with a number of extras, particularly in the detailed fittings.

DF304/5

88,000-88,010
88,250-88,633

Otherwise known as the Daimler Regency Mark II saloon, introduced in 1953. Headlamps were fitted in the wings and the engine was more powerful than the Mark I version.

DF312/3

These chassis were only used as test beds for the Hobbs automatic gearbox.

DF306/7

91,450-91,474

A more powerful development of the Daimler Empress.

DF314/5

90,100-90,234

This chassis prefix was for automatic transmission Daimler One-O-Fours.

Lanchester Leda.

DF400 & DF400/1

In 1954, the Daimler Regency Mark II was announced, a more powerful version with a 4 ½ litre engine. A number of Daimler Sportman and Hooper Empress bodies were also built on this chassis.

DF402/3

More powerful engines were produced on this chassis, but being too powerful for the gearbox, no further development was undertaken.

DF316/7/8/9

98,000-98,749 (RHD);
98,750-98,769 (LHD);
98,770-99,774 (RHD);
99,780-99,794 (LHD).

Announced in 1958, the Daimler Majestic was developed from the Daimler One-O-Four, with Automatic gearbox, further developement of the Daimler Majestic included minor changes to chassis and running gear.

LG15

A proposed upgrade of the Lanchester LA14 which never went into production.

DH27

Based on the Daimler DC27 Ambulance, the wheelbase was increased to 12'6" and Hooper Limousine bodies added. All these limousines were bought and used by Daimler Hire Limited.

Daimler Conquest.

LJ200/1

65,007-65,999 November 1951-April 1953 (RHD)
66,000-66,314
October 1952-October 1953, (LHD)
67,150-67,940 May to November 1953, (RHD)
67,948, (RHD)

These were the designations for the Lanchester Ledas and the Lanchester Fourteen. A total of 2,099 of these Lanchesters were produced.

LJ202/3

Probably the designation for the abortive Lanchester Coupé, which despite pre-production planning, was dropped prior to release. The drophead was later remodelled as a Daimler.

LJ204/5

This was probably to have been a Lanchester Roadster, but the car never got beyond the initial design drawings.

LJ252/3

Otherwise known as the Lanchester Dauphin, which was a specially bodied chassis with a Daimler Conquest Century engine downgraded to 92HP. Two cars are known to have been displayed at the 1953 Motor Show, but the Dauphin never went into production.

DJ250/1

82,500-84,999;
84,500-84,540;
85,050-87,076

Introduced in Spring 1953, this was a Daimler badge engineered version of the LJ200 range, with an upgraded engine. The Daimler Conquest was one of the more successful of the Daimler range throughout the 1950s.

DJ252/3

DJ252 87,550-87,749
DJ253 87,750-87,799

Introduced in Spring 1954, this was a four-seater convertible version of the Daimler Conquest Saloon.

DJ254/5

The two-seater Daimler DJ254 Roadster first appeared at the 1953 Motor Show. The 1955 Motor Show saw the introduction of a much improved Daimler New Drop-Head Coupé, which was a three seater. The four-seater Daimler DJ252 was dropped when then the new coupé appeared.

Daimler DJ254.

DJ256/7

90,950-91,349;
91,350-91,416;
91,700-92,699;
92,975-93,974;
95,000-95,999;
96,500-96,849;
97,050-97,303

Otherwise known as the Daimler Conquest Century, there were a number of external and mechanical differences between the Daimler Conquest and the new model. The name Century was derived from the 100HP six-cylinder engine introduced with this model.

DJ258/9

These chassis were used as a test bed for the Hobbs automatic gearbox.

DJ260/1

97,550-98,049;
98,050-98,296

Daimler Conquest Centuries fitted with an automatic gearbox.

DK400/1/2/3

92,725-92,785;
92,965-92,969;
93,700-92,724;
96,000-96,106.

This extended Daimler Regency chassis was introduced in 1954 and used for limousines and some of the Docker Daimlers ("Stardust" and the "Ivory White Golden Zebra Car") and powered by the 4 1/2 litre engine.

Hooper produced a one-off known as the Daimler Regina and Carbodies produced a version which was rather like an oversized London Taxi! Some more graceful cars were built, two of which went into Royal ownership.

LM150/1

70,100-70,112

13 Lanchester Sprites were built, and only one survivor is known to exist.

LM152/3

These numbers were reserved for other models in the abortive Sprite range.

Hooper-bodied Daimler DK400 Limousine.

DN250/1

This was the development model for a 2 ¹/₂ litre V8-engined saloon car based on the Vauxhall Cresta bodyshell.

DP250/1

This was likely to have been the Hooper designed four-seater version of the Daimler SP250.

SP250/1

10,0000-10,0005 (Prototypes);
10,0010-10,0569 (RHD);
10,0570-10,0759 (RHD);
10,0760-10,1324 (LHD);
10,1325-10,1509 (RHD);
10,1510-10,1585 (LHD);
10,2510-10,2834 (RHD);
10,3710-10,4456 (RHD).
Introduced at the 1959 London Motor Show, this two seater fibreglass bodied sports car was in volume production by the time of the Jaguar takeover in 1960. Originally designated the "Dart", this name was dropped because Dodge had already laid claim to the name in the United States. As the car was developed under Jaguar various specifications were given, A, B and C.

SP252

Experimental Daimler Mark II SP cars were built by Jaguar as an exercise, but the cars never went into production. A number of significant changes were made, and photos show Jaguar influence in both the exterior body panels and the interior of the car. By 1964, the introduction of a new Daimler sports car was not commercially feasible, given the success of the E-Type Jaguar.

SX250

This designation refers to the Ogle bodied glass fibre coupé on the SP250 chassis.

DQ450/1

DQ450: 136,701-136,710 (Prototypes);
136,711-136,890;
136,916-137,891.
DQ451: 136,891-136,915
Known as the Daimler Majestic Major, this car was powered by the Edward Turner designed 4 ¹/₂ litre V8 engine.

DR450/1

136,001 and 136,002 (Prototypes)
136,011-136,699;
139,001-139,176.
This was the Limousine version of the Daimler Majestic Major, and was two feet longer than the saloon.

The Daimler 2 ¹/₂ litre V8 and Daimler V8 250 2 ¹/₂ litre saloon

1A 1001-1A 13377
V8 250 Saloon 1K 1001 - 1K 5780 DN indicates overdrive BW indicates automatic

DS420
1M 1001- ;(RHD) 1M20001- ;(LHD)
Based on the Jaguar 420G saloon body and utilising the Jaguar XK 4.2 litre engine, this Limousine was Jaguar designed with coachwork by Vanden Plas.

The Daimler Sovereigns
4.2 (Daimler Sovereign 420)
1A 30001-1A 35476(RHD);
1A 70001-1A 70355
4.2 (Daimler Sovereign Series I)
1U 1001-1U 11894(RHD);
1U 50001-1U 50726
2.8 (Daimler Sovereign Series I)
1T 1001-1T 4069(RHD); 1T 50001 (LHD)
4.2 (Daimler Sovereign Series II - Short Wheelbase)
2M 1001-2M 3313(RHD)
2M 50001-2M 50115(LHD)
4.2 (Daimler Sovereign Series II - Long Wheelbase)
2S 1001-2S 12816 (RHD)
2S 50001- 2S 50704 (LHD)
4.2 (Daimler Vanden Plas)
3C 1001- 3C 1818 (RHD)
3C 50001-3C 50012 (LHD)
4.2 (2-door)
2H 1001- 2H 2586 (RHD)
2H 50001-2H 50112 (LHD)
3.4 (Daimler Sovereign Series III)
3B 1001-3B 3345 (RHD)
3B 50001-3B 50004 (LHD)
4.2 (Daimler Sovereign Series III)
300001 -

The Daimler Double-Six and the Daimler Double-Six Vanden Plas
Series I
2A 1001-2A 1524(RHD)
2A 50001-2A 50011 (LHD)
Long Wheelbase Vanden Plas
2B 1001-2B 1337 (RHD)
2B 50001- 2B 50005 (LHD)
Series II Long Wheelbase
2K 1001-2K2925 (RHD)
2K 50001- 2K 50227(LHD)
Series II Long Wheelbase Vanden Plas
2P 1001-2P 2220 (RHD)
2P 50001-2P 50395 (LHD)
2-Door
2F 1001-2F 1372 (RHD);
2P 50001-2F 50027 (LHD)
Series III
300001 -

Series 2 XJ-type Daimler Sovereign.

Appendix II

The Daimler & Lanchester Owners Club Limited

Founded in June 1964, *The Daimler & Lanchester Owners Club Limited* is a mutual company with a membership of approximately 3,000 enthusiasts worldwide. It incorporates *The Lanchester Register 1895-1931*, an older organisation which was affiliated in the mid-1960s. The Patrons are Mrs G Lanchester, widow of George Lanchester and Mr Alec Norman, a founder member and great supporter of the club throughout the years from its formation.

The club publishes *The Driving Member*, a monthly A4 quality magazine with a variety of articles of interest to enthusiasts of both marques.

In addition, the Club runs a stores operation which caters for a wider range of Daimler and Lanchester vehicles than any commercial organisation and has a Registrar system which provides authoritative advice and assistance to owners of most of the vehicles produced by the Daimler and Lanchester Companies. A system of Branch Secretaries organises social events and Rallies and provides support for owners in the UK, USA, Canada, Australia, New Zealand, France, Holland, Germany, Sweden and most Commonwealth countries. An informal affiliation is enjoyed with local clubs in many countries and there is a worldwide exchange of information.

Membership is by annual subscription and further details can be obtained from:

Mr J L Ridley, The Manor House, Trewyn, Abergavenny, Gwent, NP7 7PG.

Telephone 0873 890737

The Driving Member, monthly journal of the Daimler and Lanchester Owners' Club.

The Daimler and Lanchester Owners' Club is concerned with the preservation of all Daimler, Lanchester and four-wheeled BSA vehicles. As a result of efforts by its members many fine examples of the marques have been found and preserved.

INDEX

ABOUT THE AUTHOR

Tony Freeman was born in Middlesborough in 1961. His interest in cars stems from childhood, when his family owned a large dealership specialising in Austin, Wolseley and Morris.

Professionally, Tony is a Company Secretary in Public Practice in London, and a Director of a publishing company.

Over the years he has owned and restored several Daimlers, including a V8-250 and an XJ-type 4.2 Vanden Plas. Tony has also been an official of the Daimler & Lanchester Owners' Club Limited for a number of years, making him well qualified to write this book.